This Wasn't for the Public

Biodun Abudu

ALSO BY BIODUN ABUDU

Tales of My Skin

Stolen Sanity

Forbidden Scriptures

Open Letters From Within

Tea, Tips & Tricks

Tea, Tips & Tricks 2

Confessional Scriptures

Notes to Self: A Human's Journey

Public Etiquette: Uncensored

Sex Etiquette: Uncensored

Unholy Scriptures

Dedication

For the ones who smiled through survival.
Who held it all together while falling apart inside.
Who kept showing up even when no one asked how
they were doing.

For the ones who were told to stay quiet.
To not embarrass the family.
To protect someone else's comfort, image, job, or
belief.

For the truths you buried to keep the peace.
For the shame you carried that was never yours.
For the friendships, faith, and futures that didn't
survive the silence.

This book is for you.
For everything you weren't allowed to say
until now.

Prelude

This wasn't for the public.

None of this was.

It was for the group chat that went silent.
For the friend who ghosted you after you told the truth.
For the late-night text you deleted before you hit send.
For the thoughts you swallowed because you didn't
want to ruin dinner.
For the shame you've carried so long, it started dressing
like confidence.

This book is not polished for your comfort. It's not
packaged for your timeline.
It's the things we admit only after we've been broken
and sometimes not even then.

Some of these chapters will feel like your own voice
the one you silenced to keep the peace, keep the job,
keep the image, keep the family together.

Others will offend you.
Good.

That means you've still got something to unpack.
Something to unlearn.
Something to admit.

So read this knowing:
You were never meant to.
But now that you're here...

Don't look away.

Author's Note

This book draws from documented history, cultural memory, and lived experience. Some events referenced are widely recorded but rarely taught in full.

This work is not an academic text.
It is an act of witnessing.

It does not attempt to catalogue sources, but to confront truths already preserved in public record.

This work reflects personal perspective, cultural observation, and lived experience, and is not intended as a statement of fact about any individual person or event. This book is a work of literary nonfiction drawn from memory, observation, and public record, and does not claim to represent the full or definitive truth of any person, institution, or event.

Some names, details, and identifying characteristics have been changed to protect privacy.

Table of Contents

PART II: Love, Loss & Silent Grief

(The emotional wreckage we carry without eulogies)

PART III: Contracts We Never Signed

(The fine print of living in work, worth, and wage)

PART IV: Mirrors, Masks, and the Body You Wake Up In

(The identity we didn't choose, and the performance we perfect)

PART V: Systems, Silence & Sacred Audacity

(The things we weren't supposed to question and did anyway)

PART I: Flesh, Survival, and Desire

(What we give away just to feel chosen or stay afloat)

This section explores the places where need overrides intention where bodies, boundaries, and values are traded for connection, stability, relief, or survival. These chapters examine how desire, money, hunger, validation, and escape quietly reshape our decisions long before we recognize the cost. What begins as wanting often turns into bargaining, and what feels like choice slowly becomes necessity.

1.   Sex & the Cost of Hunger

(Sex, obsession and control)

The power of sex is underestimated, and little do people know it is often the reason certain things stop going right in their lives. Sex can be a spiritual hindrance, but because it feels good *too* good it becomes irresistible. It feels so good that by the time many people realize it, their body count is in the dozens...or hundreds. Maybe thousands.

Every person that enters your temple leaves something behind. They deposit parts of themselves into you their trauma, their family curses, their bad luck, their unfinished battles. Sex was meant to be intimate, but many of us have given it away to strangers whose first names we never even learned. Some of us wouldn't recognize the people from the group sex we had just a month ago.

There are soul ties attached to sex. And the consequences are often worse than STDs, shame, or even HIV. Sometimes it's inheriting someone else's padlock their curse, their stagnation, their spiritual delay, even their appointment with destruction.

Dick, whether people want to admit it or not, is powerful and dangerous. For some reason, many don't know how to act once they've had access to it.

People are intelligent, disciplined human beings... until dick enters the picture.

They say broke dick is the worst kind, the kind that makes people call off work, drain their savings, abandon logic, and rearrange their entire lives just to please it.

This power doesn't spare anyone. Gay men. DL men. Men who have been chasing desire so long their bodies are over fifty but their appetites never learned restraint. I've watched how the hunger doesn't age out it just gets louder, riskier, more reckless. What once happened behind closed doors now spills into daylight, into spaces that were never meant for intimacy but get used anyway. Street festivals. Public markets. Community events that blur into something else entirely. Boundaries dissolve. Shame disappears. And what should've remained private turns performative.

Somewhere along the way, desire stopped being personal and started becoming public spectacle. And when sex loses intimacy, it doesn't become freedom it becomes compulsion. When the body leads without discipline, it doesn't liberate you. It drags you.

Not everyone who thinks about sex a lot is addicted. And not everyone who has a lot of sex has a problem. The difference isn't frequency. It's control.

Sex obsession is when sex takes up too much mental space, but choice still exists. Desire is loud. Curiosity is active. Validation is being chased.

Sex becomes a distraction from boredom, loneliness, stress, or insecurity. It may be excessive, impulsive, or reckless at times, but consequences can still slow it down. Boundaries still exist, even if they bend.

In sex obsession, sex is driving the moment, but the person still has a hand on the wheel.

Sex addiction, or compulsive sexual behavior, is different. It's when sex no longer lives in the mind alone, but controls behavior. Days and nights begin to revolve around access. Encounters are planned. Decisions are shaped by the next rush, the next release, the next distraction. Personal values get crossed. Safety gets ignored. Shame follows, yet the behavior continues anyway.

At that point, sex stops being something that happens and becomes something that is chased.

Many people didn't know this had a name back then. It was dismissed as desire. Curiosity. Being young. Being free.

But looking back, it wasn't casual. It was compulsive.

Sex wasn't something that happened. It was something life was organized around. Lines that were once clear became negotiable. Values were bent. Peace was sacrificed. Intensity was chased even when it left emptiness behind. Connection was confused with access. Attention was mistaken for affection.

It stopped being about pleasure.

It became about escape.

When something starts costing clarity, relationships, self-respect, and emotional stability, and the reach for it still doesn't stop, that's when it becomes clear it was never just sex. It was survival dressed up as desire.

This is how obsession hides in plain sight.
This is how appetite replaces purpose.

This is how dick ruins lives quietly, publicly, and without apology.

Somewhere, a woman is sitting in a therapist's office telling a story that could be titled ***how dick ruined my life.*** Hair matted. Eyes hollow. Nerves shot. A body still breathing but a spirit already evicted. She looks like someone who didn't lose control in one moment, but surrendered it slowly, transaction by transaction, touch by touch, until there was nothing left to negotiate.

Somewhere else, a man is sitting across from a mentor, explaining how everything collapsed. Not in flames, not loudly, but through repetition. Through hunger he kept calling desire. Through nights that felt like proof of power and mornings that felt like evidence. He says "rock bottom" like it was a single event, not a long agreement he kept renewing. He doesn't mention the names. He mentions the access. The feeling of being wanted. The silence after.

Neither of them calls it addiction.

They call it love.

Or loneliness.

Or a phase.

Or freedom.

But both of them are describing the same thing:

a life reorganized around a body part and the slow disappearance of everything else.

I've seen people choose dick over friends, family, and life-altering decisions unmoved even when a loved one is in the hospital, because their only priority is making sure that dick isn't in the presence of someone else.

We've seen people who were well-raised, educated, sharp, and emotionally healthy lose themselves once toxic dick enters their lives. Suddenly they look worn down. Their sanity slips. Their common sense disappears. Decisions become reckless. Nothing else matters. The person attached to the dick becomes the one in power.

He lives rent-free.

He calls the shots.

He eats for free.

He drives cars that aren't his.

He plays his game system while you work yourself into exhaustion.

And the list goes on.

We've watched wealthy, phenomenal, influential women become thin, exhausted, and hollowed out because the dick in their lives kept them stressed. No amount of therapy helps. No advice from friends penetrates. Because the moment he says, *"Just let me put the head in,"* all power disappears.

From the tip, the whole thing enters.

And control is taken.

Her sense of direction vanishes.

We hear stories of people ending up in hospital beds after just one month of dating someone all because he said he was seeing someone else. They overdose. They collapse. And people watching from the outside never realize what they're actually witnessing: the grip of sex, the grip of attachment, the grip of unbroken soul ties.

While he sits by her hospital bed pretending to care, he's already browsing for his next victim.

We see people calling off work because of sex. Some spend entire days scrolling apps and websites, refreshing messages, chasing the next hook up work ignored, time erased, life paused until sex is secured. Boundaries disappear. Inhibitions collapse. Sexual addiction is real and many of us aren't ready to admit it. But when you're sleeping with everyone around you, spending your last dollar just to feel wanted, and panicking at the thought of not having sex, it's time to face the mirror.

At some point, obsession stops being something that happened to you and becomes something you chose not to question.

Not to shame yourself but to save your soul.

2. **Everyone Has a Price**

(Money, survival, and exploitation)

In hard times, dignity, class, and even human empathy walk out the door. Money talks and it leads the way.

In countries facing economic collapse, I've watched men who once swore never suddenly consider sleeping with other men for money, just to provide for their wives, girlfriends, or children. Survival rewrites morals quickly. Hunger doesn't negotiate. Rent doesn't care about pride.

Everyone has a price. And this is where bribery and corruption step in. Judges. Police officers. Gatekeepers. Decisions get made based on what's placed into someone's hand. Eyes turn blind when they should testify. Truth becomes flexible when eviction is near and stomachs are empty.

Survival creates markets people don't like to name. Some sell blood. Some sell sperm. Some sell access to their bodies, their time, their silence, or their faith. When the body becomes inventory, even reproduction turns transactional. What was once intimate becomes a product with a price tag.

When survival is on the line, people will do what they swore they never would: lie down for another man, take a sugar daddy or sugar mummy, betray someone they love, or trade silence for safety. Prostitution isn't the only transaction in this world. The ones who look the most innocent behind closed doors often have a number too.

Everyone is trying to make a living in a world that keeps getting harsher.

A church girl doesn't go on camera and strip on command without a price. A public fight on television wigs flying, bodies exposed after a contract is signed doesn't happen without a check attached.

Loyalty shifts when money enters the room. Morals become negotiable when survival is threatened.

Some even find religion profitable. Not because they were called but because the pulpit pays. Becoming a pastor, prophet, or spiritual leader can turn into a business model, where tithes replace wages and donations become survival. Faith gets packaged, fear gets marketed, and hope becomes a recurring payment. Not everyone preaching believes but everyone collecting understands money.

To survive the unspoken, the forbidden, and the inhuman, people cross lines including betrayal, exploitation, and sometimes even murder. Poverty doesn't just break pockets. It breaks people.

Some women intentionally get pregnant for security not out of love, but out of fear of returning to poverty. Mothers leave their children behind to dance on poles, trusting strangers to raise what they cannot afford to protect. There's no judgment here.

This is reality. You do what you have to do to stay alive.

Everyone has a price. Whether it's cash, protection, access, status, a barter deal, a pact with the devil, or an exchange for fortune and fame.

We just don't like admitting what ours is.

3. **Addicted to Escape**

(Vices, binge culture and numbing the noise)

We don't always run because we're reckless. Sometimes we run because staying still hurts too much.

I didn't realize how many ways I was escaping until I started paying attention to what I reached for the moment silence showed up. Travel. Work. Scrolling. Sex. Anything that made the noise stop even briefly. Relief became the goal, not healing.

Whether it's travel, food, sex, alcohol, work, or fantasy, many of us are running from our lives instead of living them. And the cost of chasing relief over healing is higher than we admit.

People wonder why some folks are always on PTO, always traveling, always booking trips with their last dime. What they don't realize is that travel is sometimes an escape plan. Not everyone is content with a life built around working, paying bills, and dying. Sometimes leaving your zip code isn't about luxury it's about survival. It's about escaping the crime in your country, the instability you didn't choose, the circumstances that landed on you without consent.

And when we're not traveling, we're scrolling.

We scroll through social media for hours, living through strangers. Watching their wins. Their bodies. Their timelines. Their highlight reels. We judge ourselves for not succeeding as fast as someone we've never met, yet we keep scrolling anyway because even comparison hurts less than sitting alone with our own thoughts. Entertainment becomes anesthesia. Noise becomes comfort.

While some escape work, others hide inside it. They stay at the office from 8 a.m. to 8 p.m. when the job is officially 9 to 5. Unpaid overtime. Unasked-for loyalty. They're the ones people joke about saying she needs a man, he needs a woman, they have no life. Their PTO maxes out. HR forces them to take time off. But no one asks what they're running from.

Sometimes it's abuse at home.
Sometimes it's grief.
Sometimes it's loneliness.

Others avoid family gatherings altogether. Not because they don't love their families but because they're tired of being measured. Still single. Still no kids. Still explaining their life choices like a courtroom defense. And for some women, the pain cuts deeper in cultures where motherhood is treated as proof of worth. In many African households, a wife who has not given birth is quietly reduced to a "roommate," sometimes even called her husband's fellow man, as if marriage only becomes real once children arrive or as if love only counts when it reproduces. It is even worse when there is no son to carry the family name. Love, loyalty, and partnership are dismissed, and the woman is made to feel temporary in her own home. For some, this constant erasure becomes another reason to escape, emotionally or physically, just to survive the shame placed on them.

Some people leave their families at home and sit at the bar, bottle after bottle, until numbness feels like peace. They stumble home drunk, eat whatever's closest, and pass out. Weed. Pills. Drugs. Anything that quiets the noise. Anything that helps them avoid the place they call home which, for them, feels more like hell than safety.

We're often told there's a right order to life. Love. Marriage. Kids. Career. Happiness. But we're not built the same. When life becomes unbearable, alcohol becomes a shoulder to lean on. When there's heartbreak, some of us make an emergency appointment with a bucket of ice cream. Retail therapy becomes treatment. Sex becomes distraction. Work becomes refuge.

No one fully understands another person's escape.
But we all have one.

Some escapes destroy us.
Some just keep us sane.

And the line between coping and addiction is thinner
than we want to believe.

And the truth is, not all escapes look destructive
from the outside. Some are applauded. Some are
rewarded. Some are even called "self-care." But
avoidance doesn't stop being avoidance just because
it's socially acceptable. Running doesn't stop being
running just because it's dressed up as productivity,
independence, or ambition.

Escaping doesn't mean you're weak.
It means something inside you is asking to be heard.

And until we learn how to sit with discomfort
without numbing it, we'll keep booking the trip,
pouring the drink, scrolling the feed, staying late,

buying the thing anything that lets us postpone the
moment we have to ask ourselves why we're hurting
in the first place.

Healing asks for presence.
Escape asks for permission to disappear.

Most of us were taught how to survive not how to
heal.

4. **Prescription America**

(Pills & numbness, avoidance & denied healing)

We live in a country where discomfort is treated as a defect and silence is sold as treatment. When something hurts emotionally or physically the first response isn't to listen. It's to prescribe.

I didn't question it at first. I trusted the system the way we're taught to until I noticed how quickly pain was medicated and how rarely it was understood.

When new pills come out, some of us become the test dummies. We're told it's safe, it's approved, it's progress while our livers quietly carry the cross and absorb the damage along the way. When people speak uncomfortable truths, the solution is often medication. Not to heal but to suppress.

Pills are profitable. Healing isn't always. The side effects are written so small we barely read them, and even when we do, we don't fully understand what we're agreeing to. Years later, the consequences show up in ways no one warned us about.

Natural remedies aren't promoted the same way not because they don't work, but because pills generate recurring profit. And the people who discover cures using natural methods often disappear from the conversation. Sometimes the cure vanishes. Sometimes it reappears years later with a heavy price tag, released only when desperation peaks.

From the beginning of time, humans healed naturally. There was a time healing didn't come in orange plastic containers.

It came from the ground.

Aloe. Frankincense. Myrrh. Olive. Hyssop. Fig. Pomegranate. Cedar. Mustard. Mint. Rue. Coriander. Cumin. Garlic. Onion. Balm of Gilead. Cassia. Cinnamon. Saffron. Grapes and wine.

Knowledge once carried by memory is now carried by prescription. Somewhere along the way, treatment became industry. This isn't to say all medication is evil it isn't. But many drugs come with side effects we weren't properly informed about or encouraged to question. We were taught compliance, not curiosity.

We walk around with backpacks, designer bags, and purses filled with the jingle of pill bottles Monday-to-Sunday organizers reminding us of the ten different medications we must take daily just to function. Meanwhile, the fruits that once provided vitamins are either unaffordable, inaccessible, or barely advertised. Heavily drugged has quietly become the new normal.

Cabinets are filled with medications we can't even pronounce. Every few minutes, there's a commercial for a new pill with a catchy song, smiling actors, abud side effects rushed through at the end like a legal afterthought. The harsh reality is that being sick is now expensive. A single bottle of cough medicine can cost twenty-five dollars and still not work.

What we don't talk about enough is how pills can quietly shorten life expectancy. How they damage organs. How they interfere with fertility. How they alter the body's natural ability to heal, create, and multiply. These conversations are rare but the people at the top smile, knowing the profits will last generations.

America isn't just overworked. It's overmedicated.

And numbness has become easier to sell than healing. We weren't taught how to ask better questions only how to swallow answers. So we keep medicating symptoms while ignoring causes. We keep numbing pain instead of understanding it. We keep trusting systems that profit from our silence. Healing asks for time, honesty, and discomfort. Pills ask for compliance and in a country addicted to convenience, compliance will always be easier to sell.

5. **Fed to Death**

(Food, chemicals & survival)

We live in a country where food is everywhere yet nourishment is rare. Eating should keep us alive, but somehow it's doing the opposite.

I didn't start paying attention until I noticed how often I felt tired, bloated, sick, or foggy after meals that were supposed to be "normal." That's when it hit me: we aren't eating to thrive anymore. We're eating to survive what we're being fed.

It's bad enough that the American life span keeps shrinking while fast-food chains multiply on every corner. Convenience is everywhere, but real nourishment is harder to find. Chickens, fruits, and vegetables are injected with substances designed to extend shelf life while quietly shortening the lives of the people consuming them. Food doesn't look like food anymore. Pork, lamb or chicken doesn't resemble what it once was. Chemicals are added without our knowledge, and many of us don't realize that some additives are linked to long-term illness, including cancer. Sugar is packed into everything, quietly fueling diabetes and chronic disease. We're left confused, trying to keep up with what's safe to eat when it feels like ninety percent of what's available is harming us.

Eating has become a guessing game.

Even when we try to eat something "simple," like chicken, we're not safe. Fast-food chicken is often rushed, poorly handled, and undercooked still raw on the inside, sometimes with visible blood. Speed matters more than safety. Volume matters more than health. And the customer bears the risk.

It's why the fear of potlucks is valid. Not everyone washes their hands properly. Not everyone cleans their meat correctly. Not everyone understands food safety and illness doesn't care about good intentions.

Some Thanksgiving invitations shouldn't be accepted out of politeness. Protecting your body isn't rude. It's survival.

And now even access to food has turned into a financial trap.

Delivery services promise convenience, but the bill tells a different story. Service fees. Operation fees. Taxes. Delivery fees. Tips. Sometimes even extra handling or storage charges. By the time the food arrives, you've paid double for something that may leave you unsatisfied, sick, or worse. Meanwhile, cooking at home is cheaper, safer, and often healthier. Yet for some reason, many of us run from our own kitchens even though home-cooked meals could save us money, protect us from food poisoning, and give us back control over what we consume.

We laugh at farmers. We dismiss rural life. We mock people who weren't born into city culture. Yet the same people we joke about are often the ones living past eighty eating food grown from their own land, free from chemicals, free from factories, free from constant contamination. They eat what they grow. They know what's in their food. And their bodies reflect it.

Food didn't betray us.
The system did.

Most people don't realize that 3D food printing is already a real thing. Some foods are now created using machines that print food instead of growing or raising it. In simple terms, 3D food printing takes ingredients like plant proteins, purees, or processed food pastes and builds edible items layer by layer using digital designs. These foods aren't harvested they're assembled.

The goal is efficiency, uniformity, and control control over texture, appearance, shelf life, and even nutrition. It's marketed as innovation, sustainability, and the future of food. But the farther food moves from soil, sunlight, and farms, the more disconnected we become from what we're putting into our bodies.

The problem isn't technology.
It's disconnection.

Add to that the global consumption of animals humans were never meant to eat. Snakes. Insects. Exotic wildlife. Animals taken from environments carrying diseases that transfer from species to species. When hunger meets poverty, standards collapse. Survival eating turns into sickness.

We're not just fed poorly.
We're fed carelessly.

And while corporations profit from shelf life, mass production, and convenience, the human body pays the price. Food is no longer about nourishment. It's about survival in a system that prioritizes profit over health.

We aren't just eating to live anymore.

We're living in a way that slowly feeds our own

destruction.

6. Survival Crimes

(When hunger and desperation replace choices)

When financial assistance, public aid, food stamps, or job access is taken away, people act surprised when crime rates rise. But the connection is obvious. You remove survival, and desperation fills the gap.

When there aren't enough jobs for people without bachelor's or master's degrees, theft becomes more common. Stores get robbed. Banks get hit. Not because people are born criminal but because options disappear. When legal pathways are blocked, illegal ones open.

When medicine becomes unaffordable, people don't just get sick they steal prescriptions. They grab what they need and run out the store because pain doesn't wait for policy changes. When food is taken off tables and rent is due, hunger turns into anger. Desperation turns into action.

And who can blame them?

People at the top watch millions get laid off and respond by cutting assistance even further. They make decisions from offices that will never know hunger, eviction, or choosing between heat and groceries. It's easy to debate morality when your survival has never been threatened.

This isn't about defending people who refuse to help themselves when help is available. This is about people who are trying and getting blocked. People who need temporary support to regain footing, not punishment for falling.

No one wakes up wanting to rob a store. No one dreams of being angry. Crime is often the result of being ignored, stripped of options, or pushed into corners with no exits.

Some people even commit crimes on purpose not for profit, but for shelter. Prison becomes a roof. A bed. A meal. Warmth during winter. When incarceration feels safer than freedom, something is deeply broken.

This isn't lawlessness.
It's survival with no other plan.

Until systems address hunger, housing, healthcare, and access desperation will keep replacing choice.

And somehow, there always seems to be money to support another country while our own struggles through wildfires, hurricanes, floods, and displacement. Communities burn, rebuild, and grieve while relief feels delayed and aid becomes conditional. Priorities start to look questionable when help moves faster across borders than it does across neighborhoods. But who am I to say such a thing.

7. **Lust for Likes**

(Social media & performance)

We live in a time where being seen matters more than being real and perception pays better than truth.

I didn't understand how addictive that performance could be until I watched how easily validation replaced peace.

As my fellow Nigerians would call it *fake life* is on the rise.

People are doing anything and everything to present a version of their lives that looks impressive online, all for attention from strangers and the currency of likes. They live and breathe for validation. The likes become proof of worth. Without them, the confidence collapses.

Some go to extreme lengths to keep up appearances borrowing clothes, cars, and posing in homes that aren't theirs. Photos get edited to make it seem like they woke up for breakfast in Italy, spent the afternoon shopping in Paris, and ended the night clubbing in Dubai. Comments are hidden to avoid being called out. But lies are heavy. And eventually, the pressure of maintaining an image you don't live begins to crack the spirit.

Social media is a drug.

Faces are Photoshopped beyond recognition. Bodies are reshaped until real life becomes unrecognizable. People look nothing like their profiles, and when they're seen in person, the illusion collapses. Some influencers borrow designer clothes just to return them after a photoshoot. Others trade sex for access designer bags, VIP sections, exclusive locations all so they can post content that suggests a life they don't actually have.

It's all performance.

Meanwhile, the ones who are authentic stand out without trying. They move differently. They smile differently. Their peace shows. You can tell who is living and who is acting.

Some people go broke just to feel "among." Just to post something that will make their so-called haters jealous. But when the phone is down and the lights are off, it's tears soaking pillows. Anxiety replaces applause. Silence replaces validation.

Likes don't pay rent.
Filters don't fix insecurity.
And a curated life can still be an empty one.

40

PART II: Love, Loss & Silent Grief

(The emotional wreckage we carry without eulogies)

This section speaks to the losses that never received flowers, funerals, or closure. The relationships that faded, the people who left without dying, the grief we were expected to move on from quietly. These chapters explore heartbreak, abandonment, caregiving, regret, and the unspoken mourning that follows love when it doesn't end cleanly. This is grief without ceremony carried alone, remembered privately, and rarely acknowledged.

8. **Parenthood Wasn't the Plan**

(Unspoken regrets)

Not every parent wanted the life they ended up living and that truth is rarely spoken out loud.

Some parents blame their children for not becoming who they imagined, for not fulfilling dreams that were never theirs to carry. Behind closed doors, many cry. Some think, *I wish I had waited*. Others regret not the child, but the partner they had the child with.

The cost of parenthood doesn't always arrive gently. Sometimes it crashes in. We see parents sitting at bars late into the night, drinking to escape the reality waiting for them at home, children whose cries feel overwhelming, whose needs feel endless. Some fathers leave their wives in hospital beds and go on trips with friends while their partners are left to heal alone, navigating newborns and painful C-sections without support.

Postpartum is real and devastating. It reshapes emotions, identity, and self-worth. Some parents spiral into depression so deep they begin to harm themselves, or struggle with intrusive thoughts they're too ashamed to name. They look at their bodies after birth and don't recognize themselves. They look at their lives and feel trapped.

Midnight cries break patience. The cost of raising children breaks bank accounts. Exhaustion breaks spirits. Some parents hide in bathrooms or closets just to cry grieving the version of their life that disappeared the night conception happened.

And sometimes the pressure turns violent. Some parents lash out physically in moments of rage, exhaustion, or emotional collapse. Abuse doesn't always start as cruelty it starts as untreated pain, unchecked anger, and a system that ignores warning signs. And in the most tragic cases, children lose their lives at the hands of the very people meant to protect them. We see it in the news often enough to flinch, then scroll past stories of children harmed or killed not because they weren't loved, but because the adults responsible for them were drowning and never helped.

There are parents who stay in relationships they wanted to leave the moment the baby arrived, believing sacrifice will be rewarded. They stay "for the kids," only to grow old and be placed in nursing homes by the very children they gave everything to.

Words get said in anger that can never be taken back. *I wish I aborted you. I regret the day you were born.* Even when apologies follow, there is often truth buried beneath them the truth that becoming a parent required giving up something deeply personal. And then there are stories no one wants to talk about. People who were raped and forced by law, religion, or circumstance to carry pregnancies they never chose. Parents required to stare into the face of a child who reminds them daily of violence they endured.

Single parents carry another weight entirely. Many take out their pain on their children not because they don't love them, but because they were cheated on, abandoned, and left to raise a life alone while the other parent disappeared.

This isn't about hating children.
It's about naming the grief adults are told to swallow.

Parenthood is often portrayed as unconditional joy. But for many, it's complicated, painful, and filled with regret no one allows them to speak.

And silence doesn't erase that truth.

9. **The Friendship Funeral**

(Friendship grief)

There is a thin line between a best friend, a friend, a coworker you call a friend, and someone who is really just an associate. The problem is we often blur those lines, give people titles they didn't earn, and then feel offended when they don't pour back the same energy. We expect commitment from people who never signed up for it.

We're not that close anymore.

Friendships shift. Awkward truths surface. Growing apart happens. But no one gives us a manual for how to grieve a friendship while the person is still alive.

When a friend betrays you, it cuts differently. You don't know whether to inherit their enemies or stay neutral. Ending a friendship hurts like a breakup, yet society rarely acknowledges that pain. The anger, the confusion, the silence it all lingers.

That's why we start asking who's going to be at the party before we accept the invite. Sometimes avoiding them feels easier than pretending everything is fine.

And sometimes it isn't betrayal that ends friendships it's silence during the moments we needed support the most. When life gets heavy and your friend disappears, that absence speaks louder than words.

Some friendships fade when one person gets booed up and the other is still single. When one friend gets pregnant while the other still wants nightlife. Priorities change. Lifestyles shift. Even work friendships change when someone leaves a job especially if the workplace was toxic. The person who escaped doesn't always want to relive it through constant venting.

Growing apart is uncomfortable to admit. When one person chooses peace and the other thrives on chaos, alignment breaks. When the people someone keeps around them are constantly getting arrested, living recklessly, or pulling you into situations you've outgrown, distance becomes necessary. Sometimes growth requires separation.

Some friendships also end because people lack the maturity to accept difference. Different opinions, different growth paths, different boundaries instead of allowing space, they take it personally.

What could have been understanding turns into ego. What could have been evolution turns into resentment. And rather than adjusting, they end the friendship altogether.

Sometimes friendships shift simply because someone new enters your life and you realize you have more in common with them. It doesn't erase the history you shared with an old friend, but it changes the dynamic. Growth exposes compatibility.

And sometimes friendships existed not because of deep connection, but because you shared a season, a space, or even a common enemy. Being united by resentment or opposition isn't the same as being aligned by values.

Moving to another state creates distance too physical and emotional. When you're no longer present in each other's daily lives, commitment fades. Closeness weakens.

You start thinking about the memories the nights out, the tears, the meals shared and then something as small as not being reposted or not liking a post becomes symbolic. Petty, maybe. But in this era, even silence online feels like a message.

And the hardest truth?

Some people don't know how to be friends. Not because they're evil but because they don't have enough in them to give.

Friendship grief doesn't come with flowers or closure.

Some losses don't come with goodbyes they just teach you who won't walk with you into the next season.

52

10. **Save Our Souls**

(Caregiving & depression)

Caregiving is a tough, unexpected job. Even when doctors warn you, no one gives you a manual for how to care for a sick family member who is angry, sad, or depressed because of their condition. Watching someone you love deteriorate in front of you is mentally exhausting and emotionally crushing.

Imagine your family member being hospitalized for a year. They live in another state or two hours away, and you still have a full-time job that is already toxic. You rush to make medical decisions on their behalf, leave work early to catch visiting hours, and carry the weight of knowing they may not have much time left. And corporate America still expects productivity, focus, and smiles at meetings. Hang your feelings at the door. Maybe this is why systems prefer AI, because as humans there is no way you are not haunted by the face you saw the night before. The one who could not speak. The one who could barely recognize you.

The person you are caring for may lash out. They may become mean, impatient, or cruel, even though you are only trying to help. All of this is new to you. When it happens, you excuse yourself, cry quietly in a hospital hallway, wipe your tears, and walk back into the room to continue caring for them.

Sometimes this becomes emotional abuse, even if it is unintentional. You tell yourself it is not their fault, yet you still wonder why kindness disappears when you are the one holding everything together. They are facing their mortality, and you are carrying the weight of loving them through it.

It hurts even more when your siblings disappear. When everyone quietly steps back and leaves you to figure it out alone. Suddenly, you feel like the only child. You ask for help, ask them to share time, decisions, or responsibility, and your messages go unanswered. Calls are ignored. You are left on read. The silence is loud, and the resentment builds, because caregiving was never meant to be carried by one person alone.

Siblings disappear when the work is heavy, but some suddenly reappear when there is a will to be split. Phones that never rang before start working perfectly once there is something left to claim.

Caregiving also comes with a financial toll no one prepares you for. Medical care puts families into deep debt that takes years to escape. Insurance does not cover everything, and someone is always paying the difference. It is even worse in countries where hospitals require payment before treatment. People are turned away while bleeding, injured, or dying because a deposit was not made. Families are forced to watch their loved ones suffer or die in hospital hallways. That trauma does not disappear.

The mental toll on caregivers is global. We see it on television and think it is sad, but when it happens to us, we ride trains and buses home in silence, cry in our cars, collapse into bed, and whisper prayers for strength. We ask when it will end, knowing the ending may require us to make the hardest decision of all.

Sometimes love means letting go. Sometimes it means making the call to end their suffering and pulling the plug, even when you are unsure if it is the right decision, because they can no longer communicate their wishes. That weight stays with you forever.

Caregivers grieve while the person is still alive.
And no one checks on them.

11. **Death Toll**

(Emotional numbness & invisible loss)

So many people die in tragic ways, and somehow life keeps moving as if nothing happened. There is no moment of silence. No pause. Just the noise of the world demanding we keep going. People die, and we are expected to return emails, show up to work, and continue functioning as if loss is something we can schedule around.

Some people die and are never properly buried. Bodies go unidentified after natural disasters, accidents, wars, and mass tragedies. Families never get closure. Remains are lost, misplaced, or left unnamed. And it makes you wonder how there are so few burial grounds when so many people have died across generations. Where do they all go. Are bodies stacked on top of each other. Not everyone chooses cremation. And we already know some bodies are stolen or misused for reasons never fully disclosed. The numbers do not add up, yet no one wants to ask too many questions.

With work, children, and daily responsibilities, many of us never get the space to grieve. Jobs call us back before we have processed what just happened. Bills do not pause. Schedules do not soften. Men are told to be strong and not cry when they lose a parent.

Tears are treated like weakness instead of proof of love.

Every year, tens of millions of people die across the world. Not slowly. Not quietly. On average, hundreds of thousands of lives are lost every single day. Every minute, families are being notified. Every second, someone is taking their last breath. While one household is mourning, another is welcoming a newborn. People exit as others enter. Life becomes a revolving door of arrival and departure, and we are taught to accept this rhythm without reflection.

Without ceremony. Without time to sit with the weight of it.

History shows us that countless lives have been lost to senseless wars. Entire communities erased because of pride, power, and ego. From ancient conflicts to modern ones, people die not because there were no alternatives, but because leaders refused to step back. Borders are defended. Dominance is asserted. Ordinary people pay the price.

The love of money has wiped out communities too. Villages reduced to test grounds. People treated as expendable, injected with substances they never fully understood or consented to, all in the name of progress, research, or profit. When money leads and ethics follow, human life becomes disposable.

Then came COVID-19. A period when death was no longer distant or isolated, but global and unavoidable. Death counts climbed rapidly. Loss became daily. Families said goodbye through screens. Funerals were delayed, restricted, or denied altogether. Some accepted it as a health crisis. It scared many of us. It made others suspicious. Some still believe it was more than a health crisis. A quiet reduction. A reminder of how disposable life can feel when systems fail.

Since then, death has become background noise. Headlines blur together. Loss scrolls past us daily. We absorb it, then keep going. Some of us have grown numb to life itself. We kill without thinking. We drive drunk. We poison out of jealousy. We harm out of rage. We take lives and call it an accident. We forget how fragile existence actually is.

Death surrounds us more than we like to admit.
And the scariest part is not dying.
It is how easily we learn to keep going as if it never happened.

12. **The Quiet Exit**

(Suicide & silence)

Opening poem

Suicidal

Unhappy

Depressed

Considering

Withdrawing

Ending

A bad way

to tell the whole world

"I quit"

Self-destruction

Suicide is not the answer, but not everyone knows
how to carry what they are holding. Some people

reach that edge after being shamed online, after their intimate moments are exposed, after heartbreak, bullying, abuse, or relentless humiliation. When pain becomes public and support disappears, silence feels heavier than life itself.

Teen suicide is rising, and it is devastating. Many young people are hurting in ways adults refuse to acknowledge. They are bullied, abused, neglected, and pushed into a world that demands strength without offering guidance. We are told the youth are the future, yet when they ask for help, they are dismissed. When they seek therapy or support, some are told to toughen up, stay quiet, or submit instead of being protected.

Young people look to elders for direction, hoping for wisdom, safety, and clarity. Too often, they are met with competition, jealousy, or indifference. Some adults see youth not as lives to nurture, but as threats to their relevance. Support is withheld. Doors are closed. And the silence grows.

The world has become deeply self-absorbed. Many young people feel unheard, unseen, and disposable. Some wander the streets late at night, not looking for trouble, but trying to escape homes that feel heavier than hell. Tomorrow feels uncertain. Hope feels delayed. And the truth feels guarded by those who refuse to share it.

Understanding the mind of a young person in pain is not easy, but ignoring it is deadly. Many just want someone to listen without judgment. Too often, the only attention they receive comes with conditions, exploitation, or abuse. They are taken advantage of, then mocked for being vulnerable. Labeled reckless instead of wounded.

Young people are risk-takers because they are builders. Entrepreneurs of possibility. Dreamers in a world that often tells them their dreams are foolish or unrealistic. When elders dismiss those dreams, they are not just rejecting ideas. They are rejecting lives.

God, open the eyes of the world. Let adults see the power in the youth instead of fearing it. Let them create space for young voices, put microphones in their hands, and listen. The world will soon belong to them.

If guidance existed earlier, fewer teens would feel lost. Fewer would be pregnant without support. Fewer would confuse validation with affection. Fewer would believe that disappearing is the only way to be free.

Bills pile up. Pressure builds. Shame lingers. Even wealth cannot protect against despair. We see celebrities with everything end their lives, reminding us that pain does not check bank accounts before entering.

Suicide is not strength.
Silence is not peace.
And the quiet exit leaves echoes that never fade.

What saves lives is not judgment, but presence.
Not control, but compassion.

Not silence, but someone finally saying, *I see you.*
Stay.

Support note

If you or someone you love is struggling with
thoughts of self-harm, help is available. In the
United States, you can call or text **988** to reach the
Suicide and Crisis Lifeline. It is free, confidential,
and available 24/7. If you are outside the U.S., local
crisis support services are available in many
countries.

13. **The Apology That Never Came**

(Forgiveness, closure & emotional accountability)

Forgiveness is not as common as people like to pretend. Some of us carry resentment like a second heartbeat. We ride it out until the wheels fall off. We hold grudges for years, replay arguments in our heads, rehearse what we should have said, and keep score like it's survival. For some people, the anger never cools. It just becomes part of who they are.

Closure is rarely given. Especially after heartbreak. Especially when someone wronged you and walked away without looking back. People leave messes behind and expect time to clean it up. They disappear without explanation. They move on without accountability. And the person left behind is told to heal without ever being acknowledged.

I've learned that silence from someone who hurt you can be louder than the harm itself.

A simple apology goes a long way. Not to reopen wounds, but to stop the bleeding. One honest "I'm sorry" can save years of confusion, bitterness, and self-blame. It can prevent people from making reckless choices just to numb the pain or prove they are okay. It can stop someone from questioning their worth over something that was never their fault.

Some wounds don't fade.

They ferment.

They sit in people for years, collecting names: humiliation, abandonment, betrayal, silence.

Most people turn that pain inward.

It becomes depression. Addiction. Isolation. A life lived smaller than it was meant to be.

But a few let it rot into something else.

They start rehearsing conversations that will never happen.

Apologies that will never come.

Justice that was never offered.

They don't wake up wanting to destroy anything.

They wake up wanting the pain to stop being invisible.

And when no one ever names what was done to them, when no one ever says I was wrong, when silence keeps winning...pain looks for another language.

Sometimes that language is self-destruction.

Sometimes it is withdrawal.

Sometimes it is a hardness the world mistakes for cruelty.

An apology would not have saved everyone.

But it could have interrupted the story before it hardened into something heavier.

Before hurt learned to speak in ways that only create more hurt.

Closure is not about reopening the past. It is about naming it. It is about recognizing the harm that was done and the role each person played in it. Without that acknowledgment, the hurt doesn't disappear. It just hides. It shows up in new relationships, new arguments, new fears. It becomes baggage other people never signed up to carry.

Forgiveness is often misunderstood. It is not saying what happened was okay. It is not excusing disrespect, betrayal, or abuse. Forgiveness is choosing not to let someone's wrongdoing keep controlling your future. It is deciding that your peace matters more than their pride.

Emotional accountability is the missing piece in most broken relationships. It means owning your actions without deflecting, minimizing, or rewriting the story. It means saying, "I hurt you," instead of, "You took it the wrong way." It means understanding that intentions do not erase impact.

Too many people avoid accountability because it requires humility. It requires sitting with discomfort. It requires admitting you were wrong without waiting for the other person to be wrong too. So instead, they stay silent. They ghost. They move on. And the apology never comes.

Some parents never apologize to their children. Some siblings pretend nothing happened. Some friends betray you and expect access later. Some lovers break you and act surprised when you do not heal on their timeline. And some people die without ever acknowledging the pain they caused.

When an apology never comes, you have to decide what to do with the weight. Some people carry it forever. Others learn to set it down without permission. Closure is not always given. Sometimes it is built. Quietly. Alone. With boundaries.

An apology costs nothing.

Avoiding one costs people years of peace.
And emotional accountability is not weakness.
It is the bare minimum of being human.

14. **The Loneliest Season**

(Holidays, spending & forgotten meaning)

The holiday season Christmas, Thanksgiving, New Year's, and more can be one of the most depressing times of the year. It reminds you of what you do not have. A partner. A family. Children. Stability. That reality often gets ignored because everyone around you is focused on material things, decorations, and gifts. Time is no longer valued. Presence is replaced with packages. A mailed box is considered enough, even when what someone really needed was a visit.

It becomes even harder when your birthday falls around the holidays or the day after Christmas. People forget. Or they give you one combined gift. Or they cannot show up because they already spent too much on Christmas. From Halloween to Thanksgiving to Christmas to New Year's, bank accounts are drained. That is why so many people look forward to tax season, hoping refunds will help them recover from holiday spending. Very few people feel comfortable saying I am on a budget, this is what I can afford, or I cannot buy gifts this year. Instead, they overextend themselves quietly and deal with the stress later.

Somehow, these holidays push people into debt. Thousands of dollars are spent trying to meet expectations that were never realistic to begin with. You buy gifts for family and friends who may not appreciate them and who might have preferred the latest phone over the bracelet you sacrificed your last dime to afford. They do not see the cost behind the gesture.

We participate in Secret Santa exchanges at workplaces where people do not even wish us well. We buy gifts for bosses who created toxic environments by singling us out, ignoring our efforts, and bullying us quietly all year. Yet during the holidays, we are expected to smile, show gratitude, and pretend one festive day erases months of mistreatment.

We celebrate holidays without knowing their meaning or history. Maybe it is because we are exhausted from working and paying bills nonstop. Any excuse to be off work feels like a gift. It is not like most of us live in a country designed for balance where siestas, early closings, or time to breathe are actually possible.

The saddest unspoken truth is this. We have elderly family members we do not see all year. We wait for holidays to make time for them as if love needs a calendar reminder. Visits are postponed until tradition demands them, not because connection does.

The holidays have become big business. Corporations profit while meaning fades. Parades, sales, and spending take center stage while unity, love, community, and presence get pushed aside.

For many, this season is not joyful.

It is lonely.

And no one talks about that part.

PART III: Contracts We Never Signed

(The fine print of living in work, worth, and wage)

No one sat us down to explain the real terms of survival. We entered adulthood agreeing to systems we never negotiated. Jobs that demand loyalty without protection. Wages that shrink while expectations grow. Education that promises opportunity but delivers debt. Worth measured by productivity instead of humanity. This section explores the invisible contracts we are bound to every day. The ones we never signed, yet are punished for breaking.

15. **Modern Slavery**

(Work, exhaustion & betrayal)

Work is no longer just a place we go to earn a living. For many, it has become a system of survival that quietly drains the body, the mind, and the spirit. We wake up programmed to clock in and clock out, repeating the same cycle for years, sometimes decades, with little growth and no real reward. Ten years at a company can pass and you still have not reached financial stability, even in leadership roles. Loyalty is demanded. Advancement is optional.

I've watched people give their best years to a job only to realize the system was never designed to give back.

When workers turn to Human Resources for help, they often discover that HR protects the company, not the employee. Policies change without warning. New rules appear overnight. The burden always falls on the workers who stayed while leadership watches the revolving door spin. Workloads grow heavier as positions remain unfilled, and burnout becomes normalized.

Managers claim to understand, but many have never done the job they oversee. Some earned their positions through family connections or favors, not experience. Support is promised but rarely planned. Workers cope by making memes, recording videos, and publicly admitting how toxic their jobs are. Some joke about wishing the office would burn down just so they do not have to return. Yet when applying elsewhere, they pray they are not jumping from one nightmare into another.

It is painful to watch CNA workers in nursing homes responsible for ten to twenty patients per shift. Bathing them. Feeding them. Turning them every two hours to prevent bed sores. Responding to constant call bells. These are the same workers who develop chronic back pain and health issues later in life, yet are paid barely enough to survive. DSP workers caring for people with developmental disabilities often earn as little as seventeen dollars an hour in cities like New York, despite facing physical violence, emotional strain, and unpredictable workdays.

Many workplaces reward those who flatter leadership instead of those who actually produce results. The most capable employees are ignored, overworked, and disrespected. Then leadership wonders why profits decline. Unrealistic goals are set while retention issues are ignored. Companies stop asking workers how they feel, what they need, or how conditions could improve.

Exhaustion breeds resentment. Some workers retaliate by exposing companies publicly. Others file lawsuits. Some quit without notice. Others turn to spiritual retaliation out of desperation. Surveys around the world consistently show that most people hate their jobs, especially those with no flexibility, no remote options, and no respect for work life balance.

Imagine spending eight hours a day, five days a week, surrounded by coworkers you dislike more than your own family. That kind of environment erodes the mind. It hardens people. It makes them angry, numb, and emotionally unavailable.

Layoffs happen without warning. No severance. No transition. Just panic about how to feed a family. We are told to be passionate about our nine-to-five jobs, but passion does not survive exploitation. Passion disappears when a job exists only to pay bills. For the few whose work aligns with purpose and pays well, that is a blessing. For everyone else, five o'clock is freedom. Not because they love leisure, but because work has already taken everything it could.

15B. **Work Life in the U.S vs the Rest of the World**

(Survival dressed up as success)

Work life in the United States feels like survival mode disguised as ambition. Long hours are praised. Burnout is normalized. Being exhausted is worn like a badge of honor. People are expected to be grateful just to have a job, even if that job drains their health, time, and joy.

After ten years of working for the same company, ten years of showing up, meeting goals, covering gaps, taking on extra work, and often going years without a real raise, all you are given for your anniversary is a pen with the company's logo on it. That's it. A pen. No bonus. No extra time off. No meaningful acknowledgment of the decade you gave them.

That moment tells you everything. It tells you that loyalty was never valued, only tolerated. That your time wasn't an investment, it was something to be used until it ran out. Ten years of labor, stress, missed moments, and emotional exhaustion reduced to branded stationery.

Companies will celebrate profits, quarterly wins, and growth loudly, but when it comes to honoring the people who stayed, the response is minimal by design. Longevity isn't rewarded. It's exploited. The longer you remain, the more replaceable you become.

The pen isn't a gift.It's a receipt. Proof that the system knows exactly how much it can take from you and how little it has to give back.

In the U.S., time off feels like a luxury instead of a right. Many workers don't get paid vacation at all. Sick days are limited. Parental leave is inconsistent or nonexistent. Calling out feels like a risk. Rest feels like rebellion. Even when time off exists, people are guilted for using it. You are made to feel replaceable the moment you choose your body over the company.

Healthcare workers experience this cruelty on another level. Nurses, aides, CNAs, and support staff are overworked, understaffed, and underpaid, yet expected to show endless compassion while their own bodies break down. They lift patients without enough support. They work double shifts out of necessity. They absorb trauma daily and are told it's part of the job. Many leave the profession not because they don't care, but because caring costs them their physical and mental health.

Compare that to many European countries, where work is structured around life, not the other way around. Paid vacation is standard. Four to six weeks off is normal, not rare. Sick leave is protected. Parental leave is long and supported. People actually step away from work without fearing punishment or replacement.

In some countries, the workday itself is shorter. Offices close earlier. Lunch breaks are real breaks. Time with family is protected. The goal isn't to extract every ounce of productivity from a person. The goal is sustainability. People are allowed to be human without apologizing for it.

In the U.S., healthcare is tied to employment, which turns jobs into traps. People stay in toxic environments because they need insurance. They endure abuse, overwork, and silence because quitting could mean losing access to care, medication, or treatment. Survival becomes conditional. Employment holds power not just over income, but over life itself.

Remote work exposed the truth. Many jobs didn't need offices. Commutes weren't necessary. Productivity didn't collapse. People had more balance, more rest, more time to exist. Yet instead of embracing flexibility, many companies forced people back, not because it made sense, but because control mattered more than outcomes.

In Europe and other regions, work culture often accepts that humans are not machines. In the U.S., exhaustion is still confused with dedication. Hustle culture convinces people that rest is laziness and that suffering is a requirement for success. You are taught to push through pain, ignore warning signs, and be grateful for crumbs.

The difference isn't work ethic.

It's values.

Some systems are built to support people.

Others are built to extract from them.

Burnout isn't a personal failure. It's what happens when a system takes more than it gives and uses you until there's nothing left.

15C. **Starting Tired**

(Fatigue as inheritance & Children of the algorithm)

There is a generation that did not enter the world rested.

They were born into debt before they learned numbers, into systems already strained, into families carrying financial damage that never made the news. While older generations were told to work hard and build, many of today's youth were told, quietly, to brace themselves.

They inherited the bill.

Not just student loans, but inflated rent, unstable healthcare, shrinking wages, climate anxiety, and economies that reward speed over stability.
Childhood became a waiting room for responsibility.
Adolescence became training for exhaustion.

This is not laziness. It is arithmetic.

When wages do not match the cost of living, effort becomes irrelevant. When pensions vanish and retirement becomes a rumor, urgency moves backward in time. Parents work longer.

Grandparents return to jobs their bodies have already outgrown. And children grow up watching survival replace planning.

Digital life did not soften this.

It accelerated it.

They became children of the algorithm before they became adults taught productivity before identity, metrics before meaning, branding before belonging. Algorithms taught them what to want, how to look, how to compete, and when to feel behind. Rest became suspicious. Idleness became guilt. Even play was optimized.

Burnout is no longer a phase.

It is an upbringing.

Many young people are not chasing dreams. They are outrunning collapse. They choose practicality over passion, security over curiosity, stability over selfhood. Not because they lack imagination, but because imagination does not pay rent.

And so adulthood arrives early, unannounced.

With resumes instead of questions. With side hustles instead of space. With anxiety treated as ambition.

We call this resilience.

But it looks more like fatigue passed down.

A system where survival is inherited is not opportunity.

It is quiet captivity.

And the cruelest part is how normal it has become to expect children to carry what adults built and could not fix.

They are not behind.

They were never allowed to begin.

This is not a generational accident. It is an efficient design. A population raised in debt does not ask dangerous questions. A population trained to monetize every hour does not organize. A population that enters adulthood already exhausted does not revolt, it negotiates for survival. Fatigue is cheaper than freedom. Burnout is easier to manage than hope. When children grow up calculating rent instead of possibility, when identity is postponed in favor of income, when rest becomes something you earn instead of something you deserve, control no longer needs force. It only needs bills. What looks like collapse is also infrastructure. What sounds like personal failure is actually economic inheritance, passed down quietly, reinforced legally, and protected politically. A tired generation is not a flaw in the system. It is proof that the system is working.

94

16. **Small Business, Big Barriers**

(Visibility, power & survival)

I have always questioned why platforms celebrate businesses that already have millions while ignoring the small businesses that actually need visibility to survive. The same brands are constantly spotlighted, recycled, and applauded, while struggling entrepreneurs are told to wait their turn or prove themselves in systems that were never designed to favor them.

Some platforms even create competitions for small businesses, promising funding, exposure, and support. People apply, prepare, and wait with hope. Then the winner is announced, and it turns out to be someone already connected to the platform. A friend. A favorite. Someone who never needed the opportunity in the first place. Resources circulate within the same circle, while everyone else's time, labor, and hope are wasted.

I've seen how small businesses are invited into rooms not to be supported, but to fill seats and make systems look fair.

While some criticize the idea of highlighting Black-owned businesses, the truth is more complicated. Some events labeled as Black-owned business platforms operate without professionalism or care. Vendors are charged hundreds of dollars for tables with no guaranteed crowd, poor marketing, and no real support. Emails go unanswered. Phone numbers exist but are never picked up. Organizers collect vendor fees, dance, celebrate, and perform in front of struggling vendors while rain leaks onto products and no assistance is offered during the event.

Vendor fees range from two hundred to four hundred dollars for a table and two chairs, often without proper promotion. There is no follow-up, no check-ins, no concern for whether vendors make enough to recoup their costs. It is an uncomfortable truth that even within our own communities, professionalism is sometimes missing, and accountability is avoided.

Big brands rarely go out of their way to collaborate with smaller ones. Instead, they buy space, dominate markets, and drive out businesses that existed long before them. Marketing platforms charge small businesses the same rates they charge million-dollar companies. Imagine asking a small brand to pay five thousand dollars for a single post with no guarantee of results. Meanwhile, those same platforms freely promote brands that are already popular.

Small businesses struggle to compete when large companies steal their ideas, knowing the original creators cannot afford legal protection. Many unique businesses shut down not because the ideas were weak, but because support was absent. Communities are quicker to repost trendy corporations than the local business owner trying to survive. Applications from small businesses are ignored, while large brands enter events freely because of the crowds they attract. The cost they were supposed to pay is quietly passed down to the smaller vendors.

Small business owners wear every hat. They are the marketer, the HR department, the designer, the photographer, the accountant, the social media manager, and the event planner. A single repost, mention, or genuine collaboration can change their trajectory. Visibility is not charity. It is survival.

Small businesses do not fail because they lack talent or effort. They are starved by systems that profit from their hope, invite them in for appearances, and never intend to give them real access or a fair chance to win.

17. **No One's Middle Class Anymore: The Success Lie**

(The collapse of stability)

Let's be honest. The middle class is carrying a weight that no one wants to talk about. From taxes to rising costs, the middle class is expected to fund everything while being excluded from conversations meant for the poor or the rich. Everyone talks about poverty. Everyone studies wealth. But no one talks about the people in between who are silently drowning while doing everything "right."

In simple terms, the classes used to look like this. The poor struggled to meet basic needs and often relied on assistance to survive.
The middle class worked, paid bills, saved a little, and hoped for stability.
The rich had excess, security, and options.

That structure no longer exists.

Now, poor is extremely poor. Rich is extremely rich. And the middle class is barely holding on.

The poor often qualify for assistance, food programs, housing support, and temporary relief. The rich have accountants, tax shelters, investments, and influence that protect their money.

The middle class makes just enough to be denied help, but not enough to live comfortably. They earn too much to qualify for assistance, yet not enough to breathe.

The middle class pays the highest taxes, covers the gaps in public systems, and absorbs the cost of inflation without protection. When prices rise, they are told to budget better. When rent increases, they are told to downsize. When groceries double, they are told to make sacrifices.

One unexpected bill can push them into debt overnight.

I've watched people do everything they were told, work nonstop, stay employed, avoid trouble, and still fall behind with no safety net waiting for them.

Systems are designed to protect wealth, not stability. The rich get richer because the system multiplies money once you already have it. The poor struggle to climb out because wages lag behind the cost of living. And the middle class is squeezed from both ends. Taxed heavily. Excluded from aid. Blamed for not managing better.

The middle class often works the hardest. They work full-time, sometimes multiple jobs. They carry degrees and debt. They show up every day. Yet they are one emergency away from collapse. One medical bill. One layoff. One rent increase.

There is no longer a ladder. It is no longer poor, middle class, and rich. It is now poor, barely surviving, and unreachable wealthy. Stability has become a myth sold to people who followed the rules and still lost.

The real success lie is this: that hard work guarantees security. For many, hard work now only guarantees exhaustion.

The Retirement They Promised

They promised rest at the end.

A porch. A chair. Time.

Instead, they gave people arthritis and a login portal.

Retirement became a rumor.

Not a plan.

What they called "the future" was built on wages that never stretched, pensions that quietly disappeared, and 401(k)s tied to markets that gamble with people's last good years. It was sold as security, but designed like a cliff. So now seventy-year-olds wear name tags. They push medication carts. They stand behind registers. They clock into nursing homes as CNAs, lifting bodies while their own joints burn. They answer corporate emails with hands that should have been resting. Not because they want to, but because rent does not care about age. Insurance does not honor exhaustion. And their children, buried under debt, rent, and survival, cannot afford to carry them. So parents return to work to avoid becoming a burden in a system that already made them disposable. This is what "success" looks like when the ending is removed. A life spent producing, and an old age spent proving you still deserve to exist.

The poor aren't planning for retirement.

Survival takes everything they have.

The future is a luxury when the present is on fire.

The rich don't "retire."

They already live in safety.

Their money works even when they don't.

Rest is built into their lives.

The middle class is the only group raised to believe
in retirement as a finish line.

They were told:

Work hard now.

Suffer responsibly.

Delay joy.

And one day you get to rest.

So when retirement disappears, it doesn't just hurt
financially.

It shatters the story they organized their whole lives around.

That's why it hits the middle class the hardest.

They didn't just lose money.

They lost the ending.

And the most dangerous part of all is how quietly this collapse is happening, while the middle class is told to keep smiling and keep paying.

18. **Buried in Debt**

(Credit, capitalism & quiet despair, personal & national debt)

People live in debt and die in debt. Credit cards are handed out like candy. Swipe now. Worry later. Somewhere between groceries, rent, brunch, and emergencies, debt becomes background noise. Something you carry so long it starts to feel like part of your body.

There is always something being advertised that you have no business buying. Something you are told you deserve. And when money is tight, there is always a friendly voice saying, "Just put it on your credit card. You can pay it later." Later never comes. Interest does.

Missing a due date does not just cost a fee. It multiplies the problem. Interest stacks quietly, daily, invisibly. If you do not pay the statement balance in full, the debt grows even while you are trying to shrink it.

People make payments for years and still owe more than what they started with. That is not carelessness. That is math designed against them.

Countries themselves arc buried in debt, owing trillions while still funding wars, bailouts, and global power plays. Meanwhile, regular people are told to tighten their belts, work harder, and be grateful. Assistance disappears when you need it most. Relief is conditional. Debt is permanent.

Debt sneaks into everything. Entertainment. Food. Housing. Transportation. Emergencies. Even rest. People go into debt just to feel normal for a weekend. A dinner. A birthday. A moment of relief. Then Monday comes with interest.

Debt delays life. It delays marriage. Delays children. Delays rest. Delays healing. People stay in jobs that drain them because quitting is too expensive.

They stay in relationships that hurt because separating finances feels impossible. They keep showing up exhausted because debt does not allow collapse.

More than half of adults carry credit card debt, and millions are trapped under interest rates so high their balances barely move no matter how much they pay. This is not bad discipline. This is a system that feeds on patience, shame, and silence.

What makes debt cruel is how ordinary it has become. Everyone owes something, so no one talks about it. People laugh over brunch, split the bill, and smile for photos while quietly calculating how many paychecks it will take to erase last month's joy.

Debt is not a personal failure. It is a structure. A quiet cage built with glossy cards and friendly promises.

And by the time most people realize the door is locked, they have already been living inside it for years.

19. **The Cost of Controlled Knowledge**

(Debt, education & controlled truth)

Education is one of the most profitable businesses in the world, yet it's sold to us as salvation. From a young age, we're told that school is the only way out, the only path to success, the only proof of intelligence. What they don't say out loud is how expensive that path is, and how selective the knowledge along the way can be.

No one told us the lesson would end, but the bill wouldn't. We signed up to learn, not to owe forever.

Education is controlled. What we learn is filtered through approved curriculums, edited history, and narratives the system is comfortable teaching. Certain stories are highlighted. Certain truths are buried. Certain groups are celebrated while others are summarized, erased, or softened.

We're taught what to remember, what to forget, and what not to question. Whether history is truth, half-truth, or convenience, most of us won't know in our lifetime.

People go through years of schooling, graduate with pride, and still never work in the field they studied. Degrees sit on walls while bills sit on tables. Student loans follow people into their thirties, forties, and sometimes the grave. People are still paying for education long after the lessons stopped serving them. Every year, people hope for loan forgiveness, student debt relief, or cancellation, praying the system might finally show mercy. Sometimes there are pauses. Sometimes there are small reductions. But for most, the debt remains.

So the question becomes how does it make sense to spend decades paying for an education that didn't guarantee stability, security, or even employment. A lot of what we aren't taught in school ends up being learned later. Through the internet.

Through social media. Through late-night searches that come with surprise and shock. Financial literacy. Real history. Power structures. Survival skills. Emotional intelligence. None of that was prioritized, yet we're punished later for not knowing it.

Education costs are outrageous. Families spend tens of thousands on K–12 schooling. Universities can cost seventy to eighty thousand dollars or more. Even with financial aid or FAFSA, the remaining balance still turns into loans that quietly shape people's lives. Decisions get delayed. Families get postponed. Homes go unbought. Freedom gets deferred.

This is why some people choose trades instead. They skip traditional education and learn skills that generate income immediately. Plumbing. Electric work. Construction. Certifications. Hustles built on experience instead of debt. Some become entrepreneurs. Some survive off common sense, street smarts, and resilience. For a few, that path works and they escape student loans entirely.

But let's be honest. Most high-paying jobs still require degrees. Credentials still gatekeep opportunity. So unless someone breaks through as an entrepreneur, lands a rare opportunity, or has generational support, the debt follows.

Not everyone carries this burden the same way. Some people had scholarships. Some had their education funded through programs, group homes, or state assistance. Some graduated debt-free. Yes, that exists. But it's not the majority story. Most people are carrying loans quietly, pretending it's normal, pretending it's fine.

Education was supposed to be empowerment.
For many, it became a lifelong invoice.

Knowledge came with interest.
And curiosity came with a payment plan.

20. **Privacy Isn't Private**

(Data, consent & digital surveillance)

This chapter scares me because the more you live, read, and pay attention, the more you realize that nothing is truly private anymore. Calls feel listened to. Messages feel monitored. Emails, texts, social media DMs, cloud storage, search history. Everything feels accessible to someone, somewhere.

We sign paperwork we don't read. We click "agree" without slowing down. In exchange for convenience, we hand over our privacy, our habits, and pieces of our lives without fully understanding what we're giving away.

Consent isn't really consent when the alternative is exclusion. Don't agree and you can't work. Don't agree and you can't access services. Don't agree and you're locked out of modern life. So we comply, not because we understand, but because resistance costs too much.

Street cameras. Facial recognition. Voice recognition. Fingerprints. DNA samples. Drones. Location tracking. Data collection that goes far beyond what's actually needed. We give access to information that has nothing to do with the service being offered, yet we approve it anyway because we want the app, the job, the account, the benefit.

When your body becomes data, privacy stops being abstract. Your face unlocks doors. Your voice verifies identity. Your fingerprints confirm access. Your blood confirms compliance. At that point, privacy isn't personal anymore. It's biological.

People joke about pigeons being cameras, about birds watching us from rooftops. Whether man-made birds exist in labs or not almost doesn't matter. The truth is simpler and more unsettling. Surveillance doesn't need feathers. We carry it willingly in our pockets. We unlock it with our faces. We agree to it without reading. While we laugh at flying cameras, our phones track our location, our voices, our habits, and our patterns in real time. The danger was never hidden. It was accepted.

It's not just about being watched anymore. It's about being predicted. What you'll buy. Where you'll go. Who you'll vote for. What risk you represent before you even act.

Fighting for privacy is not about having something to hide. Freedom is being able to exist without being monitored, recorded, analyzed, or sold. Freedom is being yourself without someone else controlling the narrative of your life.

Data is watched from everywhere, allegedly even from outer space. Cameras are on streets, in buildings, at work, in stores, at intersections. Your data is sold to companies. Your address, date of birth, phone number, and history live online without your consent because at some point, someone collected it and passed it along.

Once you enter government systems, you're there forever. Health records. Employment history. Addresses from years ago. Forms asking where you lived seven years back. Everything archived. Everything retrievable. Everything permanent.

Privacy didn't disappear overnight.
It was signed away slowly.
And by the time we noticed, opting out was no longer an option.

PART IV: Mirrors, Masks, and the Body You Wake Up In

(The identity we didn't choose, and the performance we perfect)

This section looks at the quiet negotiations we make with ourselves every day. The bodies we inherited. The identities projected onto us. The versions of ourselves we learned to perform just to survive, to be loved, to be accepted. It explores how self-image is shaped by expectation, shame, culture, desire, and survival, and how many of us spend our lives trying to make peace with reflections that were never ours to design. This is about what it costs to live in a body that's constantly judged, edited, policed, or misunderstood, and the long work of reclaiming who you are beneath the mask.

21. **The Body I Never Asked For**

(Body Image & shame)

It's wild how we admire a baby's body when they're born. The chubby cheeks. The soft stomach. The thick legs. We kiss what we later punish. We celebrate what the world eventually teaches them to hate. Little do we know that the same body parts we once called cute will later be the reason that child cries in bathrooms, avoids mirrors, skips school, or learns how to laugh at themselves before someone else does.

From slim to thick. Fat to curvy. Gaps in teeth. Height. Nose shape. Flat buttocks. Lips. Skin tone. Hair texture. Every body becomes a target eventually. Every feature becomes a flaw in the wrong room.

What makes it worse is when the feature is hereditary. When you look in the mirror and see your mother's nose. Your father's body shape. Your family's genetics written all over you. And instead of pride, resentment grows. People get angry at their parents for what they passed down. Angry for the weight. Angry for the hips. Angry for the skin. Angry for the bone structure. As if the body is a curse someone handed you without permission.

Now add social media. Magazines. TV. Music videos. Perfect bodies everywhere. Filters. Edits. Angles. Bodies that don't exist in real life. Faces that don't wrinkle. And suddenly people feel like they have to erase themselves to be worthy. So they cut into themselves trying to become acceptable. Some get injections in basements. Some fly overseas for fat transfers. People do BBLs (Brazilian Butt Lifts) that don't match their thighs. Faces get pulled, filled, frozen, and altered until identity disappears. And some people die in the process, all because strangers laughed under a post or a comment went viral.

People come home and stand in front of mirrors they avoid. Laughter replays in their head. Insults echo. Screenshots live forever. Sleep becomes difficult. Self-love disappears. Some ask God why He didn't make them attractive. Some wake up and go to bed in makeup because they're afraid their partner won't love the natural version of them. Afraid the real face will be rejected. Afraid the body they wake up in isn't enough to keep someone.

There aren't enough spaces that celebrate natural bodies. Natural aging. Natural features. Most examples pushed into our eyes are perfection or illusion. So people spend their last money trying to "fix" themselves, believing beauty is the way out of being overlooked, unloved, or abandoned.

And sometimes the cruelty doubles. They do all the surgery. Spend all the money. Risk their life. And it still doesn't look right. One side is uneven. Something feels off. And now the same people they were trying to attract avoid them completely.

And then there is pregnancy.

A body that already does not feel like yours becomes public. Hands touch. Strangers comment. Doctors speak over you. Laws decide. Your stomach becomes conversation. Your choices become debate. Your pain becomes background noise.

You are no longer a person first. You are a vessel.

And when the baby arrives, the body that carried life is expected to disappear quietly. Shrink back. Recover fast. Be grateful. Be silent. Loose skin becomes shame. Stretch marks become jokes. Weight becomes failure.

The miracle is celebrated. The woman is edited out.

Another body you never asked for.

Most of us weren't taught how to live inside our bodies. We were taught how to apologize for them.

This is the body you wake up in.

Not the one you asked for.

Not the one you designed.

A body judged before it's understood.

Edited before it's loved.

Policed before it's protected.

They laughed first.

They commented next.

They sold you a fix last.

A flaw became a market.

An insecurity became a business model.

You weren't born hating your reflection.

You were trained to.

Your shame was never accidental.

It was engineered.

And someone is still profiting from it.

22. Flags Down, Lights Off

(Queer identity & pride fatigue)

Support for the LGBTQ community has become seasonal. Loud in June. Silent the rest of the year.

While some people genuinely support the community, many are performative. They are the same ones cracking jokes like "LGBTQRSTUVWXYZ," reducing real lives, real struggles, and real bodies into punchlines. The same ones who say "love is love" when it is convenient but disappear when queer people actually need protection, advocacy, or backup.

Every June, companies suddenly remember queer people exist. Rainbow flags are dusted off from storage. Disposable flags. Temporary banners. Pride logos slapped onto websites, products, and email signatures. They sponsor floats, post statements, and sell Pride merch at a markup. Not because it is personal, but because it is profitable. Pride becomes a marketing strategy. Identity becomes branding. Survival becomes a campaign.

Then July arrives.

The flags come down.

The logos revert.

The lights go off.

No statements when anti-LGBTQ laws are passed. No outrage when queer people are attacked, fired, bullied, or erased. No protection when queer employees are discriminated against behind closed doors. Suddenly it is "too political." Suddenly it is "not the right time." Support is postponed until next June.

There is also the version of support that treats queer people like accessories. The "gay best friend" idea. As if having one queer person in your circle is proof of being progressive. Some people want proximity to queerness without any concern for the reality of it. They want the humor, the style, the energy, the aesthetics, but not the struggle. Not the trauma. Not the stories. Not the weight that comes with living openly in a world that still punishes difference. Being wanted as an accessory while your pain is ignored is not support. It is consumption.

That false support shows itself fastest when alcohol enters the room or when emotions get heated. People who were "cool" suddenly are not. The mask slips. The slur comes out casually and carelessly right in your presence. The word *faggot* lands like a reminder that the respect was never real. That acceptance was conditional. That the moment they are angry, drunk, or triggered, your identity becomes ammunition. No apology fixes that. No explanation erases it. Because you do not accidentally say what you do not believe.

That is where the fatigue comes in.

Pride fatigue is not about being tired of being proud. It is about being tired of being used. Tired of watching corporations profit off queer culture while offering no real protection, no policy changes, and no accountability. Tired of seeing rainbow branding without healthcare benefits. Visibility without safety. Inclusion without risk.

Queer people do not get to clock out of their identity on July 1st. There is no switch to turn it off. No break from judgment. No pause on family rejection, religious condemnation, workplace bias, or violence. Pride does not end when June ends. Life does not.

Being visible one month a year does not make me feel celebrated. It makes me feel scheduled.

When the flags come down and the lights go off, what is left is the truth. Support that only shows up when it is trendy was never support at all. It was branding disguised as allyship. Love without sacrifice. Inclusion without responsibility.

If your support disappears when it stops being profitable, it was never meant to protect us.

It was only meant to look good.

And queer lives deserve more than good optics.

23. **The Third Face**

(Identity , masks, and the self we bury)

I believe every human being carries three faces.

The first is the one we present to the world.

Polished. Controlled. Acceptable.

The version designed to survive public spaces, jobs, social settings, and expectations.

The second face is the one we allow friends and family to see.

Still edited. Still protected.

This is where we soften slightly, where some truth leaks through, but never enough to make anyone uncomfortable or alarmed.

Then there is the third face.

The one no one really sees.

Not coworkers. Not family. Not lovers.

Sometimes not even ourselves.

This third face lives behind closed doors and locked thoughts. It holds what we learned to hide early. Fear. Shame. Rage. Desire. Doubt. Grief. Curiosity. Vulnerability. Longing. Resentment. Unfinished wounds. Unspoken truths.

For some people, the third face is not evil.

It is guarded.

It exists because the world was not safe enough to hold it.

For others, it is darker.

It carries impulses they learned to suppress, thoughts they learned not to voice, behaviors they learned to conceal. It is not always violent or malicious, but it can be. History shows us what happens when the third face goes unchecked, unexamined, or fully unleashed.

Most people are not hiding because they want to deceive.

They are hiding because exposure once came with consequences.

The third face often forms as protection.

But protection, when left unacknowledged, can turn into isolation.

Silence.

Distance.

Duplication.

This is how people become strangers to themselves.

We see it when someone is praised publicly but collapsing privately.

When someone appears gentle but harbors quiet cruelty.

When someone seems confident but is driven entirely by fear.

When someone is loved for a version of themselves they no longer recognize.

The danger is not that the third face exists.

The danger is pretending it doesn't.

Because what is buried does not disappear.

It waits.

It leaks into decisions.

It shapes relationships.

It sabotages intimacy.

It distorts morality.

It finds outlets when pressure builds.

Everything hidden eventually looks for air.

Some people confront their third face.

Others build entire lives to avoid it.

And that is where the real fracture happens.

Because the longer the third face is ignored, the more power it gains.

Not loudly.

Quietly.

Patiently.

Most people are not afraid of being seen. They are afraid of being seen accurately.

The most unsettling truth:

The third face does not ask for permission.

It arrives when control weakens.

Under stress.

Under desire.

Under exhaustion.

Under silence.

And by the time it shows itself, the damage has usually already begun.

24. **What They Do to Women**

(Praised for beauty, punished for desire - dissected, judged & forgiven last)

Women have carried the weight of the world since the beginning of recorded history, yet history rarely gives them the microphone. Even in the Bible, women are present but often unnamed, reduced, or remembered only in relation to men. Their stories are shortened. Their voices edited. Their suffering spiritualized instead of acknowledged. They are central to the narrative but rarely centered in the telling.

From early on, women are taught their place. Be quiet. Be agreeable. Be useful. Be desirable, but not demanding. Be nurturing, but not needy. Be strong, but never threatening. Cook. Clean. Care. Lay down. Open your legs when expected, but never ask for pleasure in return. The moment a woman speaks up, she is labeled difficult. Emotional. Aggressive. A bitch.

Historically, women were traded as property, married off as children, exchanged for land, alliances, or peace. Their bodies were currency. Their silence was safety. Their obedience was survival. Laws were written about women without women present. Religions were interpreted by men who benefited from women's submission. Medicine dismissed women's pain as hysteria. Violence against women was normalized, ritualized, and excused as discipline, tradition, or love.

For thousands of years, women gave birth upright.

Close to the ground.

Close to their bodies.

Close to control.

Then the body was turned into a surface.

Beds arrived.

Not for comfort.

For access.

For hands that were not invited.

For eyes that wanted authority.

For systems that needed a better angle.

So birth was laid flat.

Legs opened.

Gravity dismissed.

Instinct rewritten.

What was once guided by women became managed by strangers.

What was once survival became protocol.

They called it progress.

But progress that requires submission is not care.

It is discipline.

And discipline, when practiced long enough, learns how to call itself normal.

Women are praised until they speak. Desired until they refuse. Celebrated until they set boundaries. From the moment a woman enters the world, her body is watched, weighed, judged, and negotiated. Beauty is rewarded. Silence is preferred. Obedience is expected. And the moment she steps outside what is comfortable, acceptable, or controllable, the punishment begins.

When women ask for equality, the response is rarely support. Instead, they are told to prove themselves under harsher conditions. Lift what the man lifts. Endure what the man endures. Perform twice as well for half the recognition. Feminism, which at its core asks for fairness, dignity, and autonomy, somehow becomes offensive to men who confuse equality with loss of control. To some, feminism sounds like accusation instead of survival.

Women are admired like dolls but discouraged from having opinions. Desired for their bodies but dismissed for their minds. Celebrated for beauty while being punished for desire. A woman who owns her sexuality is shamed. A man who does the same is applauded. Men cheat and ask for forgiveness. Women cheat and are erased. Men are allowed to stray and return. Women are expected to be loyal even to betrayal.

In the workplace, women are called emotional for caring. Weak for expressing concern. Dramatic for setting boundaries. They are told to smile more while carrying workloads heavier than their job descriptions. They are expected to lead gently, correct quietly, and endure endlessly. When they burn out, they are replaced without reflection.

A woman can work herself into exhaustion and still be questioned. A man can show up halfway and be praised for leadership.

Women are the literal passage into this world. Every human enters life through a woman's body. And yet that same body is controlled, legislated, debated, and disrespected. Across cultures, races, and borders, women face violence, silencing, and dismissal. And within that reality, Black women carry an even heavier burden. Often described as strong to justify neglect. Expected to endure without complaint. Last to be protected. Last to be believed. Last to be forgiven.

Women are dissected from childhood. Their bodies monitored. Their aging mocked. Their choices questioned. Too thin. Too thick. Too loud. Too quiet. Too ambitious. Not ambitious enough. Mothers are judged. Women without children are interrogated. Those who choose themselves are shamed. Those who sacrifice themselves are forgotten.

Even women who remove themselves entirely from men are not spared. Lesbians are still sexualized, challenged, and disrespected by male entitlement. Their identities are treated like dares. Their boundaries like jokes. Their autonomy like something to be corrected. Some men speak about lesbian women with conquest in mind, not curiosity. Not respect. Not restraint. This is not desire. It is domination. A woman's sexuality is only respected when it centers men. When it doesn't, it becomes something to punish.

Even the most intimate decisions are rarely left to women alone. Men sit in rooms deciding whether women should be allowed to abort pregnancies. Men debate laws about bodies they will never inhabit. Men vote on whether a woman should be forced to carry a child conceived through rape. The violation happens once. The punishment is lifelong. And somehow, the conversation centers morality instead of survival. Control instead of care.

Religion has often been used as a weapon instead of refuge. Scripture filtered through male authority. Stories told selectively. Obedience emphasized over dignity. Women taught to endure instead of escape. To forgive instead of protect themselves. To stay silent instead of survive. Even in faith, women are asked to carry suffering quietly and call it virtue.

History has documented women as muses, helpers, temptresses, caretakers, and warnings. Rarely as leaders. Rarely as whole. Rarely as autonomous. When women fight back, they are labeled radical. When they retreat, they are forgotten. When they break, they are blamed.

Men could have multiple wives.

Women could not have multiple husbands.

The arrangement was called tradition, morality, and sometimes even divine order. It is amazing how often the rules seem to benefit the people who created them.

And still, women rise every morning. They build. They nurture. They lead. They survive systems that were never designed with their safety or success in mind.

A woman's strength is often praised only when it benefits others.

The darkest truth is this.

Women are celebrated for endurance, not protected from harm.

They are admired for surviving what should never have been imposed on them.

Society does not reward women for being human.

It rewards them for being quiet, compliant, and consumable.

And until control stops being mistaken for tradition,

until silence stops being mistaken for peace, women will continue to pay the highest price for simply existing.

Not because they are weak.

But because the world learned early how much it could take from them and never learned when to stop.

And when women finally stop shrinking, stop explaining, stop performing, and stop asking permission, the world calls them dangerous.

Not because they are wrong.

But because they are no longer controllable.

That is the real fear.

25. **The Isms We Swallowed**

(Racism, sexism, ageism, colorism)

This is a hard chapter.

So brace yourself.

This is for anyone who wonders why we hurt so deeply.

Why we fight so loudly.

Why we protect our culture, our holidays, our language, our skin.

Why we refuse to tolerate racism disguised as ignorance, humor, or "jokes."

This is for those who were never taught what was done to us.

And for those who were taught just enough to stay comfortable.

Racism Was the Blueprint

Racism was not subtle. It was theatrical. It was public. It was deliberate.

Black people were not simply enslaved. They were experimented on, commodified, bred, tortured, displayed, and destroyed in ways history books still soften with polite language.

People were auctioned like furniture. Families were split as entertainment. Bodies were branded with hot irons. Skin was burned, cut, whipped, mutilated. People were chained for days without food or rest. Forced to work until collapse. Punished for learning to read. Punished for looking at the wrong person. Punished for existing.

Some were tied to moving cars and dragged through towns while their skin peeled from bone. Some were forced to dig their own graves. Some were beaten while their wounds were split open and rubbed with pepper, turpentine, lime juice, brick dust mixed with lard. Dogs were unleashed to tear people apart alive.

People were suspended beneath fires. Locked into hogsheads. Smoked alive. Shackled face-down to the ground. Forced onto treadmills until death. Castrated. Amputated. Branded. Mutilated. Burned.

Children were not spared. Babies were used as bait to lure alligators. Black infants were fed to crocodiles so wallets, shoes, and goods could be made. Bodies were hung from trees and left to rot as warnings.

Strange Fruit

Strange fruit was not metaphor.

It was flesh.

Lynching was not hidden. It was communal. Crowds gathered. Photos were taken. Postcards were made. Trees that were meant to symbolize life became instruments of death. Blood soaked roots while towns went on with their day.

Bodies swinging from branches were messages.

Warnings.

Lessons.

Billie Holiday sang what textbooks refused to teach:

"Southern trees bear a strange fruit, blood on the leaves and blood at the root."

People still ask why we haven't moved on.

As if trauma obeys calendars.

Sexism Was Built In

Sexism was never separate from racism. It was embedded in it.

Enslaved Black women were exploited in ways that crossed race and gender simultaneously. Women were raped, impregnated, punished further by jealous enslavers' wives, and still forced to labor through pregnancy.

Enslaved women were routinely forced to breastfeed white children in a practice known as wet nursing. They were denied the right to nurse their own babies, who were often left unfed, neglected, or given unsafe substitutes. Many died.

These women were advertised for sale or rent, their bodies and milk evaluated like livestock. Punishments were issued if they allowed both children to feed from the same breast. Motherhood was stolen while being demanded.

"Mother" became a verb, not a bond.

Mammy dolls were created to normalize this theft. A smiling Black woman feeding white children, stripped of grief, rage, and humanity.

Sexism did not end with slavery. It evolved.

Women were told to stay behind the stove. To cook. To clean. To submit. Female rulers were questioned simply for existing. Women with voices were labeled problems. Women with power were feared.

A woman who speaks up is called emotional.

A man who does the same is decisive.

Colorism Was Engineered

Colorism was not accidental. It was designed.

Lighter skin was rewarded. Darker skin was sent to the fields. Proximity to whiteness became currency.

The brown paper bag test determined access to churches, schools, jobs, social clubs, and safety. If your skin was darker than the bag, you were excluded.

The Comb Test

Alongside the paper bag test was the comb test.

A fine-tooth comb was run through a person's hair. If it snagged or could not pass through, that hair was deemed unacceptable. Thick coils, kinks, and natural textures were treated as problems. Hair texture became character evidence.

Too "nappy" meant too unprofessional.

Too African meant too much.

These tests trained people to police themselves. To bleach skin. To scrub knuckles, knees, arms raw with chemicals. To avoid the sun. To hide during daylight. To delete photos. To straighten, relax, burn, and press hair into submission.

Bleaching causes cancer.

But so does inherited self-hate.

Featurism Took Over

Straight noses. Looser curls. "Good hair." "Better speaking."

Features were ranked.

Even Black men with natural blue eyes or lighter features were treated differently. Head light, body dark. Favoritism wrapped in denial.

Relaxers burned scalps. Bleach ate through skin layers. "Black is dirty" was taught without words.

Names were erased. Reading and writing were illegal. Education was controlled. Knowledge was rationed.

Ageism Is the Silent Trap

Ageism discards people quietly.

Workers in their 50s and 60s are pushed out. Too old to hire. Too young to retire. Experience dismissed. Loyalty punished. Retirement no longer guarantees safety.

People work longer, harder, and still face instability.

The Aftermath

All of this worked together.

Racism taught who was disposable.

Sexism taught who should submit.

Colorism taught who deserved access.

Ageism taught who was finished.

These were not accidents.

These were systems.

Trauma does not end when laws change.

It ends when truth is told.

When you know what they did to us, you understand why we fight so hard to love ourselves.

Why we march.

Why we scream.

Why silence feels violent.

This was never just about picking cotton.

This was about public torture, spiritual warfare, and generational terror, all justified as economics, tradition, or law.

The laws changed.

The trauma did not.

Understanding history is not about assigning guilt to people living today. It is about recognizing the systems that shaped the world we inherited.

And until the violence is named without comfort, until the truth is told without trimming, the isms we swallowed will keep resurfacing.

Not because we are broken.

But because history was never healed.

PART V: Systems, Silence & Sacred Audacity

(The things we weren't supposed to question and did anyway)

This section confronts the systems that quietly shape our lives while insisting we stay grateful, obedient, and silent. It examines how power hides behind policy, tradition, labor, debt, healthcare, education, and respectability and how questioning those structures is often treated as rebellion instead of self-preservation. These chapters are about breaking the spell of silence, naming what was normalized, and reclaiming the audacity to ask why things are the way they are. Not to be disruptive but to survive to see clearly, and to refuse compliance with systems that profit from our exhaustion.

26. **God Don't Like Ugly**

(Religion & rejection)

They said all were welcome.
But when people walked in, they were treated like
contamination.
Like pain needed disinfecting.
Like certain stories required silence before they
could be allowed inside.

They didn't say, "You can't stay."
They just made sure belonging felt unsafe.

Religion was supposed to be a refuge.

A place to breathe. A place to heal. A place to be held
when life gets too heavy.

Instead, for a lot of people, it became another
courtroom.

Another place where pain is measured. Where mistakes are ranked. Where suffering gets explained away as weakness. Where love is conditional and belonging has fine print.

We were told God is love.

But what we were shown was judgment.

We were told God forgives.

But what we received was surveillance.

Church can teach you how to hide before it teaches you how to heal. It teaches you what not to say. How not to dress. Who not to love. How not to exist too loudly. It teaches you quickly that honesty is dangerous and questions are disrespectful.

Sometimes the betrayal is quieter.

You tell a pastor your story in confidence. Your fear. Your mistake. Your survival. Your worst moment. You think it is safe because it is sacred.

Then Sunday comes.

And suddenly your life is in the sermon.

Not your name, but your details.

Not your face, but your sin.

Not your healing, but your wound.

They call it being "moved by the Spirit."

They call it testimony.

They call it warning.

But it feels like exposure.

Your pain becomes a lesson.

Your private shame becomes public medicine.

Your story becomes a weapon, polished into
scripture.

And you sit in the pew, shrinking, while the room nods.

Learning what happens to people who tell the truth.

Over time, people stop needing chains or threats.

They learn to monitor each other.

Correct each other.

Shame each other.

Enforce the rules on God's behalf.

Religion has been used as a weapon longer than it has been used as shelter.

Scripture was once read aloud to justify slavery.
Verses were used to defend segregation.
Pulpits taught women to submit to violence.
Churches told the poor their suffering was holy.
Systems learned early that if fear sounds like God, people will obey it.

That is why so many wounds wear halos.
That is why control learned how to quote scripture.

So people master the performance.

Hands lifted.

Eyes closed.

Pain tucked away neatly behind "I'm blessed."

Some of the most broken people sit in the front row every Sunday.

"God don't like ugly," they say.

But they never agree on what ugly is.

Ugly becomes poverty.

Ugly becomes queerness.

Ugly becomes depression.

Ugly becomes addiction.

Ugly becomes anger.

Ugly becomes doubt.

Ugly becomes surviving something you were never supposed to survive.

Suddenly, suffering is treated like a character flaw.

People will look you dead in the face and say "come as you are" then spend the whole service trying to edit you. Come as you are, as long as you do not show up too human. Come as you are, as long as you are quiet about what you lived through. Come as you are, as long as you do not embarrass the building.

When religion says "all are welcome" but looks at you like your pain is contagious, that's not holiness. That's control.

A lot of rejection in church is not loud. It is polite. It is spiritual. It comes wrapped in concern.

They will not say "we do not want you here."

They will say "we are praying for you."

They will say "God is working on you."

They will say "watch your spirit."

They will say "I'm just telling you because I love you."

They will say "I don't judge, but..."

And that "but" will be the blade.

Shame culture is one of the most effective forms of control because it convinces people they are the problem for reacting to harm. It trains people to apologize for bleeding. It trains people to feel guilty for asking questions. It trains people to confuse silence with faith.

People are told to pray harder instead of being helped.

To fast instead of being protected.

To forgive instead of being safe.

To endure instead of escape.

Abuse gets called a test.

Trauma gets called a lesson.

Silence gets called faith.

And if you leave, they say you were never serious about God.

If you stay and break, they say you lacked discipline.

Religion can turn survival into sin.

People are treated like projects, not people. Tolerated, not embraced. Welcomed, but only if they stay small. Only if they repent loudly. Only if they hide the parts that make other people uncomfortable.

There is a special kind of rejection reserved for the ones who do not fit the image.

LGBTQ people get welcomed in theory but punished in practice. Smiles in the hallway, sermons in the pulpit. "We love you" in the lobby, "we don't agree with your lifestyle" in the pews. People are told God loves them while the church makes sure they never feel safe enough to belong.

Single mothers are watched like cautionary tales.

Divorced people are treated like failures.

People who are open about sex get labeled dirty.

People who are poor get treated like they lack faith.

People who are depressed get told it's a spirit.

Everything becomes spiritual except accountability.

And the saddest part is this: some people did not lose their faith because they wanted to rebel. They lost it because they got tired of shrinking to be spared.

Some pastors become gatekeepers instead of shepherds.

Some churches become businesses instead of sanctuaries.

Some sermons become weapons instead of medicine.

Money is collected loudly.

Pain is handled quietly.

People are told to give more, serve more, volunteer more, suffer more, and stay grateful while they are breaking. Their needs are treated like interruptions, but their tithes are treated like requirements.

Churches will protect reputation faster than they will protect people.

There are places where abusers get covered, victims get questioned, and the wounded get disciplined for having wounds. Where the person who harmed someone gets "restored" publicly, but the person who got harmed gets told to forgive privately.

Forgiveness becomes a shortcut for accountability.

Grace becomes a gag order.

Confession is encouraged.

Healing is optional.

You can bleed as long as you do it privately.

The deepest damage is not that people leave religion.

It is that many leave believing God rejected them.

They don't just lose a church.

They lose their sense of worth.

They lose safety in their own thoughts.

They lose the right to question without shame.

They lose the ability to separate God from the people who spoke in His name.

Some still pray, but quietly.

Some still believe, but cautiously.

Some stop believing in everything.

Not because they wanted to sin.

Because they were tired of being crushed and told it was love.

Religion taught people to fear their own humanity and call it holiness.

And fear dressed as holiness is one of the most powerful tools of control.

People are not running from God.

They are running from being bruised in His name.

Faith should not feel like emotional exile.

The darkest truth is this.

Many people were not pushed away from God by rebellion.

They were pushed away by believers.

Not by sin.

By shame.

Not by doubt.

By rejection.

Not by wickedness.

By systems that learned how to quote scripture while breaking spirits.

If God is love, then love should not feel like punishment.

And if God don't like ugly, then what do we call the hands that bruise in His name, the mouths that condemn in His name, and the doors that close in His name?

Because that kind of ugly has emptied more souls than any sin ever could.

174

27. **The Bible Wasn't Neutral**

*(Used to control behavior through fear, morality &
selective interpretation)*

The Bible has been translated, edited, reassembled,
debated, divided, and republished more times than
most people realize. Old versions. New versions.
Removed books. Added footnotes. Rewritten
language. Softened words. Sharpened warnings.

And yet we are often told to believe it arrived
complete. Untouched. Perfectly preserved.

Somehow written by human hands, but free of
human influence.

I still wonder how the people who wrote it were able
to describe moments they never lived in.
Conversations they never heard. Thoughts they
never held. Events before memory. Before witnesses.
Before language itself had fully formed.

Maybe faith explains that.

But power explains the rest.

This chapter is not saying the Bible is evil. This is not an argument against God. It is an argument against what people do in His name.

It is saying the Bible has never been taught neutrally.

It has always passed through human authority.

And human authority always edits what threatens it power.

For centuries, scripture has been shaped less as a spiritual guide and more as a behavioral manual.

Not to free people, but to regulate them.

Not to encourage curiosity, but to enforce obedience.

Not to equalize humanity, but to rank it.

Fear became the most reliable sermon.

Some verses were elevated. Others were buried.

Some sins were magnified. Others were forgiven quietly.

Some people were disciplined. Others were protected.

Questions became rebellion.

Doubt became danger.

Silence became holiness.

Forgiveness was demanded from the wounded, not the powerful.

Love was preached, but control was practiced.

That is why "all are welcome" never feels true in real life.

Because the invitation often comes with conditions.

Believe this way.

Live this way.

Dress this way.

Love this way.

Suffer quietly.

Do not disrupt the order.

Morality became a fence.

And scripture became the wood.

Over time, people stopped needing chains or threats.

They learned to monitor each other.

Correct each other.

Shame each other.

Enforce the rules on God's behalf.

Religion has been used as a weapon longer than it
has been used as shelter.

Scripture was read aloud to justify slavery.

Verses were used to defend segregation.

Pulpits taught women to submit to violence.

Churches told the poor their suffering was holy.

Systems learned early that if fear sounds like God, people will obey it.

That is why so many wounds wear halos.

That is why control learned how to quote scripture.

Across centuries, the pattern repeated.

Those in power found verses that supported their grip.

Those in pain were given patience instead of protection.

Those who questioned were labeled dangerous.

Those who obeyed were called faithful.

Faith itself did not create this system.

People did.

And then they taught generations to confuse discipline with devotion.

Spirituality became surveillance.

God became a witness used to scare people into silence.

Many were not driven from belief by sin.

They were driven out by rules that crushed their breath.

By shame disguised as guidance.

By love that only existed if they stayed small.

They did not lose God.

They lost safety.

They lost the right to be human without explanation.

They learned that belonging was rented, not given.

That forgiveness was selective.

That holiness looked a lot like fear.

And still, the system called it righteousness.

The scripture did not build the cage.

But it was used to teach people how to decorate it,

and thank God for the bars.

182

28. **Questions from the Beginning of Time**

(Spiritual doubt, forbidden questions & biblical contradictions)

Some questions do not come from rebellion.

They come from paying attention.

From listening too closely.

They are whispered.

Passed between friends.

Thought in silence.

Buried in sermons.

Laughed off as dangerous.

Some questions survive centuries because no answer is strong enough to bury them. These are the questions people have carried for generations.

The ones faith discourages.

The ones curiosity insists on.

Not to destroy belief.

But to understand it.

This chapter is not about certainty.

It is about the thoughts people learn to swallow.

The doubts that form quietly.

The questions that echo longer than sermons.

I. The First Contradictions

Why didn't God forgive Adam and Eve?

We are told God is mercy. But the first mistake became a lifetime sentence for every generation after.

Why do we call God a man?

If we were made in God's image, and God made women, then God is not male or female, but a force.

If God sees everything, why didn't He stop the snake?

Was it a test. Or a setup.

Why is God called loving, but also a jealous God?

The same book warns us not to envy... and praises a God who does.

If Mary conceived without intercourse, why do we allow that possibility only in scripture?
In the past it became faith.Today it would become doubt.

What really happened before "let there be light"?

Was there nothing.

Or just nothing we were told.

How high was the Tower of Babel really...if today's buildings rise higher than anything before it?

Was it about disobedience...

or containment?

Was Lilith truly Adam's first wife and, if so, what else was edited out to make obedience easier to teach?

Some stories disappear not because they are false, but because they are inconvenient.

If Adam lived 930 years, what if human life was shortened on purpose so no one could live long enough to remember the truth, challenge the story, or expose what changes over time?

We outlive our questions, but not our systems. Short lives reset the witnesses before memory becomes dangerous.

II. The Stories That Don't Sit Right

Why does the Bible include incestuous relationships like fathers with daughters and brothers with sisters, yet still function as a moral guide defining boundaries for later generations?

It appears without warning, explanation, or moral weight in stories that shape entire belief systems. Sometimes it is condemned. Sometimes it is ignored.

Sometimes it becomes the foundation of bloodlines we are told are holy.

Was it really an apple that got Adam and Eve in trouble... or was the "fruit" a metaphor for sex?

What if the first sin wasn't disobedience, but intimacy and the story of the apple was written to soften it?

Was the forbidden fruit food... or flesh?

And if humanity began with Adam and Eve, were we not all brothers and sisters first?

If it was necessary at the beginning, why is it called evil later?

And how many "sins" were once survival, renamed only after power stabilized?

If the Bible mentions creatures like Leviathan and Behemoth, and many ancient cultures wrote about dragons, why is it hard for some people to accept that dinosaurs existed when we have physical evidence of them?

It seems faith accepts monsters in scripture but hesitates at fossils in the ground.

If Adam and Eve had daughters, why are their names missing while their sons are recorded?

Humanity continues through women, yet history remembers men.

Why are there no female angels mentioned?

Messengers of God are always described as male.

Power, authority, and proximity to heaven given one shape.

Never hers.

If fallen angels slept with human women, how were human bodies able to carry Nephilim?

We are told angels created giants with human women.But if Nephilim were massive, unnatural beings, what kind of body could survive giving birth to one? Was the story symbolic...or is the biology the part we were never meant to question?

Why was the Book of Enoch removed?

Why are some books "inspired" and others dangerous.

Why do angels in the Bible look nothing like how they are portrayed today?

We are shown soft faces. White robes. Calm wings. Human beauty.

But scripture describes something else.

Wheels within wheels.

Bodies covered in eyes.

One body. Four faces. (Human, Lion, Ox and Eagle)

Creatures that do not turn.

That burn.

That terrify.

If angels were never meant to look human,

why were they rewritten to be familiar?

And what else was softened, so we would not fear the truth?

We're told what God says, but no one knows how the pyramids were built?

Certainty is selective when it serves power. Faith is detailed, history is convenient, and some truths are preserved only so others can be buried.

III. Geography That Feels Guarded

When did maps stop showing the world... and start editing it?

What gets erased never argues back.

If the firmament was only symbolic, why does it have windows?

And if it was literal, how do meteoroids pass through it?

If the Garden of Eden was real and no one knows where it is, does that mean we haven't explored every corner of the Earth...

or that some places are hidden from ordinary sight? or could it be that we are no longer holy enough to see it with ordinary sight?

Did Eden disappear from the world...

or from human permission to see it?

And if it once existed, why does the Earth no longer admit where it was?

Symbols don't need architecture. Why does the firmament have windows?

Why does the Bible describe it as separating waters above from waters below, and later say it was opened during the Flood?

"All the fountains of the great deep burst forth,

and the windows of the heavens were opened."
(Genesis 7:11)

Why does the flood arrive not only from rain,

but from boundaries breaking above and below?

Symbols do not open.

Metaphors do not have windows.

**If the Alaska Triangle is real, why are its
numbers whispered instead of counted?**

When does "missing" become "myth," and who gets
to stop looking?

If 20,000 people did not vanish, why does the
number refuse to die?

And who benefits when the dead are called mysterious instead of neglected?

Is North Sentinel proof that humanity doesn't know how to mind its own business, that even clear boundaries are treated like invitations, and that "leave them alone" only becomes sacred after it's written in arrows and isolation?

Seems like humanity confuses curiosity with entitlement.

Why does the Bible begin and end at the Euphrates river?

Birthplace and grave.

Origin and warning.

And when the water disappears, so does whatever was holding things back.

Why is there still no bridge between Europe and Africa, when human beings have crossed oceans and space?

Difficulty explains delay.

But silence suggests design.

If the Ark of the Covenant was hidden for a reason, are we prepared for what happens when it is revealed... and would the world survive what we were never meant to uncover?

Do we reject giant trees because they never existed, or because nothing living today helps us imagine them?

I wonder what secrets does El Yunque rainforest hold?

Silence isn't the only way land keeps secrets.

If the Earth's shape is settled, why are the edges treated like secrets?

It does seem like maps end where permission begins.

Why is Antarctica guarded like a secret instead of a continent?

Nothing guarded this hard is empty.

Nothing.

No borders.

No ownership.

No free access.

Military permission required to visit "nothing."

That doesn't feel like science.

That feels like containment.

Why is Antartica the one place on Earth where countries that can't agree on anything suddenly agree on everything?

Permission is the language of borders.

And borders are only drawn around something that matters.

What is beyond Antarctica's ice shelves?

Maps end where certainty becomes inconvenient.

And curiosity is only dangerous when answers already exist.

If Area 51 is only about aircraft testing, why do so many people insist something else is hidden there?

Why is the Appalachian region so dangerous, and what really dwells in those mountains?

Not all disappearances are accidents. Some are revisions.

What if inner earth isn't a myth, but proof that humans are not the dominant species... just the visible one?

Every planet has layers.

We only rule the skin.

What happens when everything melts?

Not the planet.

The ice.

If most of Earth's ice melts

Antarctica. Greenland. The glaciers.

Sea levels rise by 65–70 meters.

Are we prepared?

Seas rise.

Cities sink.

Islands vanish.

Millions move.

Not from war.

Not from disease.

But because land becomes ocean.

Wars over land that still breathes.

Mass migration.

Civilization does not end instantly.

It becomes unrecognizable.

They aren't stopping it.

They're slowing it.

Artificial snow.

Reflective blankets.

Underwater walls.

Building walls.

Studying collapse.

Practicing survival.

We call it climate change.

But it's really a question of who gets protected and who is allowed to disappear.

What year does a city become unsafe before the world admits it?

God promised not to drown the world again.

He didn't promise we wouldn't do it to ourselves.

They do not need to hide the disaster.

They only need to outlive the people it reaches first.

Some build.

Redesign their land.

Cut emissions aggressively.

Transform energy.

Rebuild infrastructure.

Plan migration.

Fortify coasts.

Others rehearse speeches.

IV. Earth's Hidden Rooms

**Why have we explored only 5% of the ocean?
And what kind of life stays buried so deep
that disturbance might be irreversible?**

Some doors stay closed not because they are locked...

but because no one is ready for what listens behind
them.

**Why is the Appalachian region so dangerous,
and what really dwells in those mountains?**

Too many people vanish there for patterns to be accidental.

Too few cases are ever closed.

Are the disappearances in the Bermuda Triangle real?

Water keeps secrets better than land.

Why is Mount Kailash really forbidden to climb?

Could sacred be another word for restricted.

Why is most of the Grand Canyon off-limits?

Preservation decides what survives.

Permission decides who gets to see it.

If Africa is splitting in half, why do so few people know?

How many countries will be reshaped before the maps are updated?

When a continent breaks apart,

who updates the maps...

and who decides when the story becomes official?

V. Knowledge That Wasn't Supposed to Travel

What if the truth was never hidden... only placed in plain sight?

Could it be camouflaged as entertainment, buried in headlines, and looped until it sounds like coincidence.

How did mermaids get different names in every culture... but keep the same shape?

Different names.

Same half-human, half-sea being.

Why do gods from cultures that never met carry the same thunder in their hands...

and how did Thor and Ṣàngó become the same god in different languages?

Is the Mandela Effect rewriting history in real time?

Memory changes quietly.

Records follow later.

Why do so many ancient cultures describe a lost advanced city beneath the sea?

Did it ever exist... or was it removed?

Did Atlantis sink...

or was the ocean just where the evidence was buried?

Why do pyramids exist all over the world?

Knowledge seems travels farther than people.

Even when history pretends it didn't.

Why do ancient caves share the same drawings?

Different cultures.

The same symbols.

The same stories carved into stone.

VI. Science That Feels Like Theology in Disguise

Why is it that UFO sightings almost never come with clear, high-quality footage?

or are the cameras lowered in quality before the truth can be recorded?

Have humans truly left Earth... or just the story we were given?

Because distance is easy to fake.

Authority is harder to question.

Why do inventions that threaten powerful industries rarely survive long enough to change the world?

Some ideas don't fail.

They get buried.

VII. Power, Control & the Language of God

If King wrote a book about demons before authorizing the Bible, could he really be trusted with God's words?

Holy words still pass though human hands.

Why are questions treated as sin?

Could it be because curiosity threatens hierarchy.

Why is doubt punished faster than cruelty?

Could it be because doubt spreads.

VIII. Questions That Refuse to Die

**Why are the 6th and 7th Books of Moses
filled with spells, spirits, and the dead…**

when the Bible says his story was already complete?

**Why can't the devil just apologize so the
world can return to the Garden of Eden?**

Why was the great flood necessary?

Could it be that starting over requires fewer

witnesses? or Erasure is easier than repair.

Some questions are not meant to be answered.

They are meant to expose where obedience was chosen over understanding.

Where faith replaced curiosity.

Where silence became sacred.

And where people were taught that not knowing was safer than asking.

Questions are dangerous in systems built on obedience.

Did Giants Exist... or Was Goliath Just Convenient?

We were taught the story of David and Goliath as children. A small boy. A giant warrior. Faith defeating fear. If giants never existed, why does scripture mention them more than once, even naming the Nephilim in Genesis?

Leviathan is remembered. Behemoth is remembered. Why does Ziz fade when the monsters of scripture are named? Some stories are remembered loudly. Others are allowed to fade quietly.

Is every extinction natural?

When one tree can carry many different fruits, how many impossibilities exist only because we have never witnessed them?

Why does the Moon landing remain one of the most doubted achievements in modern history?

Whose time is actually correct? The world says one year. Ethiopia says it's years behind. No one is wrong. Time wasn't universal. It was coordinated.

29. **The Things We Don't Say Out Loud**

(Taboo beliefs, spiritual shadows & the unseen)

Some subjects make rooms uncomfortable.

Not because they are false.

But because naming them gives them shape.

There are things people joke about.

Things they whisper about.

Things they swear they do not believe in.

And yet every culture built language for them.

Every civilization has its version.

Different words. Same practice.

Influence without consent.

Africa knew it.

Europe practiced it.

The Caribbean preserved it.

Asia recorded it.

The Americas inherited it.

Not as myth.

As warning.

I. The Practices

(How people interact with the unseen)

Some people do not believe in spiritual battles.

Others believe quietly.

And some organize their lives around them.

There are attacks that leave no bruises.

Wounds that do not bleed.

Influence that never touches skin.

Dreams become entry points.

Sleep becomes a border.

Three in the morning becomes a pattern.

While cities rest, someone is always awake.

Planning.

Watching.

Speaking names into silence.

Witchcraft.

Voodoo.

Spells.

Hexes.

Curses.

Rituals.

Spirit work.

Love potions.

Different languages. Same intention.

To bend another will.

To rewrite desire.

To reroute luck.

To pull outcomes closer.

To push enemies into shadows.

Some houses do not feel empty even when
abandoned.

Some buildings were raised on cemeteries and called
progress.

Some boarding homes sit on layered bones and
locked stories.

Concrete does not cancel memory.

Children stare at corners adults refuse to
acknowledge.

Dogs bark at empty doorways.

Infants laugh at nothing the room can explain.

People call it imagination.

But imagination does not leave fingerprints on sleep.

II. Spiritual Warfare

(What happens when bodies rest)

Some battles do not announce themselves.

They arrive as fatigue.

As confusion.

As repetition.

A face that keeps appearing in dreams.

A voice that does not belong to memory.

A fear with no address.

Influence without touch.

Violence without evidence.

The cleanest wars leave no blood.

Only patterns.

III. The Currency

(What it costs)

Nothing moves without payment.

Blood offerings.

Blood money.

Wealth that arrives without a story.

Success that cannot explain itself.

Money that behaves differently than money.

Families rise too fast.

Fall too quietly.

Illness enters houses where doctors find nothing wrong.

Pain lives in bodies that test clean.

People fade inside perfect scans.

Doctors run out of language.

Medicine runs out of reach.

Some blessings rot the ground they stand on.

Some fortunes breathe heavily at night.

Sudden wealth often asks for silence in return.

And silence is expensive.

IV. Sickness With No Name

There are illnesses that arrive without diagnosis.

Conditions no machine can translate.

The body stands upright.

The spirit collapses.

Families whisper.

Neighbors pretend not to notice.

People die slowly inside bodies that appear intact.

Not every sickness is physical.

But every sickness demands payment.

V. Places That Remember

Land records everything.

Before walls.

Before ownership.

Before language.

Some spaces collect unfinished stories.

Homes that shift moods.

Rooms that alter behavior.

Buildings where joy never stays long.

Cemeteries become foundations.

Graves become basements.

Memory becomes architecture.

Silence is not the only way land keeps secrets.

VI. Possession & Attachment

(Not the movie version)

Not all possession foams at the mouth.

Some possession whispers.

A personality that changes too cleanly.

Compulsions that do not belong to childhood.

Habits that arrive fully formed.

Objects that feel heavy for no reason.

Jewelry that outlives its owners.

Furniture that travels through generations carrying moods.

Inheritance is not always genetic.

Some things are passed through silence.

VII. The Seduction

(Why people say yes)

No one begins wanting darkness.

They begin wanting relief.

Desperation.

Jealousy.

Poverty.

Revenge.

Fear of being ordinary.

Love that is not returned.

The hunger to control fate.

When doors refuse to open, people search for windows.

When effort fails, shortcuts glow.

Power is always attractive to the powerless.

And control feels holy when fear is loud enough.

VIII. Why Wc Don't Talk About It

Because belief has consequences.

Because speaking names gives them weight.

Because people would rather call patterns
coincidence than admit influence.

Because sanity is easier to protect than truth.

So language is softened.

Witchcraft becomes culture.

Curses become coincidence.

Possession becomes personality.

Blood money becomes luck.

Over time, people stop needing chains or threats.

They learn to monitor each other.

Correct each other.

Shame each other.

Enforce the rules on behalf of what they cannot see.

Silence becomes the safest ritual.

Some things do not disappear when ignored.

They only become quieter.

Patient.

Older than language.

And far more organized than belief.

The unseen does not need worship.

Only permission.

30. **Televised Programming**

(How TV raised us, distracted us, and quietly shaped our beliefs)

Before teachers.

Before textbooks.

Before life explained itself.

There was a screen.

While parents worked long hours and survival demanded their attention, the television stayed home with us. It taught us how to speak. What to wear. What beauty looked like. What families were supposed to sound like. What success resembled. What foods were "normal." What danger looked like. What love was shaped like. What kind of bodies were worthy of being seen.

It did not just entertain us.

It introduced us to ourselves.

We learned accents from characters.

Confidence from laugh tracks.

Romance from scripts.

Violence from commercials disguised as stories.

Fear from the news.

Desire from images we were too young to question.

Television did not ask who we were.

It told us.

It taught children how to sit still for thirty minutes.

How to crave what interrupted their favorite show.

How to measure their worth by applause that wasn't
real.

How to recognize themselves only when reflected back through someone else's lens.

It raised generations in living rooms while calling it "background noise."

It trained attention.

It trained hunger.

It trained comparison.

It trained obedience to rhythm.

Commercial.

Show.

Commercial.

Show.

Repeat.

And slowly, quietly, it became authority.

Not because it shouted.

But because it stayed.

**We learned how to see ourselves from a
screen that never knew our names.**

It never knew our homes.

Our fears.

Our neighborhoods.

Our languages before translation.

Our bodies before editing.

Our stories before stereotypes.

Yet it taught us what to admire.

What to chase.

What to mock.

What to hide.

What to believe was possible.

It didn't raise us with hands.

It raised us with images.

Children's Cartoons: The First Lessons

Before we could spell, we could recognize heroes.

They were thin.

Light-skinned.

Straight-haired.

Loud in courage.

Quiet in complexity.

Villains were darker.

Accents were jokes.

Mothers were absent.

Fathers were weak or missing.

Wealth was invisible but always present.

Cartoons taught children which faces were safe.

Which voices were funny.

Which bodies were worthy of love.

Which stories mattered.

They taught desire before literacy.

Hierarchy before history.

And belonging before truth.

By the time we learned to read, we had already
learned who deserved to be centered.

The News: Fear With Good Lighting

Then came the news.

A voice that spoke slowly.

Graphics that moved quickly.

Disasters framed like weather.

It taught us what to fear.

Who to blame.

When to look away.

It showed suffering until it became scenery.

War until it became routine.

Poverty until it became background texture.

It did not ask us to understand.

It asked us to accept.

And when stories repeated long enough, they stopped sounding like choices and started sounding like facts.

This is where fear stopped being information and became atmosphere.

Because once fear enters through a screen, it does not feel like manipulation. It feels like awareness. It feels responsible. It feels like staying informed.

We were trained to stay alert to disasters we could not control, crimes we would never encounter, and threats that were statistically rare but emotionally loud. Sirens became background music. Panic became posture. Anxiety became normal.

A population that is constantly afraid does not think clearly. It reacts. It consumes. It waits for the next warning.

Fear became programming.

Not loud.

Not obvious.

Just constant.

And over time, we stopped asking whether we were safe.

We only asked what we should be afraid of next.

Celebrity, Loyalty, and Borrowed Power

There is a new kind of loyalty that does not come from relationship, history, or shared risk. It comes from screens. People threaten strangers over celebrities who do not know their names. They defend billionaires like blood relatives. They mistake proximity to fame for identity. What looks like devotion is often displacement. A life without power borrowing power. A person without recognition attaching themselves to someone who is seen by millions. It is easier to protect a famous stranger than to examine your own emptiness. Easier to fight for someone else's image than to build your own. This is not love. It is emotional outsourcing.

A hunger for belonging fed by faces that will never look back.

Race, Beauty, and the Price of Being Seen

Television chose its favorites early.

Lighter skin meant leading roles.

Smaller bodies meant romance.

European features meant elegance.

Everything else became "character."

Children learned this without being told.

They learned it by who survived the story.

Who got kissed.

Who was saved.

Who was erased.

Capitalism smiled while doing it.

It sold insecurity back to the insecure.

Confidence to the unsure.

Worth to the unseen.

It taught us to purchase our way into acceptance.

New face.

New body.

New hair.

New life.

Same emptiness.

The Real Lesson

Television did not make us violent.

It made us numb.

It did not make us shallow.

It made us hungry.

It did not erase culture.

It replaced it with packaging.

It did not steal childhood.

It rebranded it.

And the coldest truth is this:

By the time many of us realized we were being shaped, the shape was already permanent.

Not molded by family.

Not grounded in community.

Not protected by truth.

But programmed.

We mistook repetition for reality.

Visibility for value.

Noise for knowledge.

And what programs you first usually owns you the
longest.

Not loudly.

Not brutally.

Quietly.

Daily.

In color.

240

31. **Lyrics We Didn't Hear**

(Music's messages, frequencies, and the things we memorized before we understood)

Music reaches us before language finishes forming.

Before bills.

Before heartbreak earns its name.

Before we understand what sex costs.

Before we own our lives.

Some of us were still borrowing our parents' toothpaste, singing about forever.

Most of us learned heartbreak before we ever held a hand.

In childhood bedrooms.

On borrowed headphones.

Singing pain we had not earned yet.

We memorized grief while still using our parents'
toothpaste.

Music reached us early.

Earlier than experience.

Earlier than language for what we were feeling.

We learned pain in chorus.

Desire in repetition.

Confidence in hooks.

Cruelty in rhythm.

We mouthed words we didn't understand yet.

Moved our bodies to stories we hadn't lived.

Practiced emotions we hadn't earned.

We sang about betrayal before we knew what trust cost.

We sang about bodies before we knew how to inhabit our own.

We sang about forever before we understood time.

Sometimes we did not even hear the words clearly.

But our bodies learned them anyway.

Hips moving to stories we had not lived.

Mouths shaping promises we did not understand.

Hearts rehearsing futures we had not chosen.

Music does not wait for comprehension.

It enters through repetition.

Through rhythm.

Through the part of the mind that opens before judgment forms.

Some songs made us feel powerful.

Some made us feel beautiful.

Some stitched us back together during nights we could not explain.

Others taught us how to disappear into desire.

How to mistake hunger for freedom.

How to turn pain into performance.

You could be fifteen, singing about betrayal.

Sixteen, memorizing how to leave.

Seventeen, rehearsing loneliness.

Sometimes the lyrics were soft lies.

Sometimes they were violent prayers.

Sometimes they were instructions dressed as melody.

And still, we called it harmless.

The Industry Behind the Sound

Music is art.

But it is also product.

And products are designed to move units before they move souls.

The industry studies hunger.

Loneliness.

Insecurity.

Sex.

Anger.

Status.

Then sells them back as songs.

Heartbreak becomes a genre.

Trauma becomes a playlist.

Revenge becomes an anthem.

Self-destruction becomes aesthetic.

The more unstable the listener, the more loyal the
consumer.

Pain keeps people streaming.

Desire keeps them buying.

Comparison keeps them scrolling.

Pain is profitable.

Sex is marketable.

Rebellion is packaging.

The industry does not sell songs.

It sells emotional templates.

How to mourn.

How to desire.

How to measure your worth.

How to be wanted.

How to be empty.

Sadness with a hook.

Anger with a chorus.

Love in three minutes.

Artists are brands.

Trauma is content.

Identity is aesthetic.

And the more universal the wound, the more
scalable the sound.

Capitalism doesn't need music to be evil.

It just needs it to be profitable.

So the sound is polished.

The beat is addictive.

The message is quiet.

And the lesson slips in underneath.

Capitalism learned what religion always knew:

Repetition is belief.

Melody is memory.

And what enters without resistance stays longest.

The Angel Who Knew Music First

Scripture says Lucifer was an angel.

Not a soldier.

Not a general.

A musician.

A leader of worship.

A voice in the choir.

The Bible never names him "angel of music."

But the idea survived anyway.

A belief passed down quietly.

That heaven trusted him with sound.

With rhythm.

With the architecture of praise.

If that story is true, then it means something uncomfortable:

Music was never neutral.

It was always powerful enough to carry belief.

To move emotion.

To bend attention.

To pull devotion.

Some traditions say his greatest weapon was not fire.

It was beauty.

That seduction works better than force.

That harmony disarms the mind.

That what enters as pleasure does not feel like invasion.

So when people say some songs feel different (heavy, addictive, hollow, hungry) they aren't always being dramatic.

Some sounds do not just entertain.

They enter.

They settle.

They repeat until they become internal language.

They teach people how to ache.

How to want.

How to hate themselves quietly.

Not through force.

Through familiarity.

Whether myth or metaphor, the message is the same:

The softest doors are the hardest to guard.

The Songs We Avoid

Everyone has a song they skip.

Not because it is bad.

But because it remembers them too well.

A car ride.

A body.

A version of yourself that did not survive.

Music does not just play memory.

It stores it.

And sometimes reopening a melody feels like
reopening a wound that learned your name.

Time makes the lyrics clearer.

Experience translates what melody once hid.

We realize too late what we had been practicing.

What We Really Learned

Music did not ruin us.

It rehearsed us.

It trained emotion before consequence.

It normalized longing.

It romanticized damage.

It made chaos feel poetic.

It gave loneliness a rhythm and called it connection.

We learned how to suffer beautifully.

How to ache on beat.

How to bleed in key.

By the time we questioned the message, the melody was already part of our thinking.

Not because it was evil.

But because it was constant.

The Quietest Truth

We thought we were choosing songs.

But most of the time, the songs were choosing us.

Entering without permission.

Staying without resistance.

Teaching us how to feel before we knew what we were feeling.

What we desire.

What we tolerate.

What we call love.

What we call normal.

We learned how to feel from songs written by strangers, sold by corporations, memorized before we understood what they were training us to become.

The most powerful message never announce themselves as lessons.

They arrive as something you hum.

Not violently.

Not loudly.

But beautifully. On beat.

256

32. **Spells We Speak**

*(The power of words, self talk, language, silence,
and the worlds we build by accident)*

Most people think language is harmless.

Just sound.

Just habit.

Just noise we use to explain ourselves.

But words are not decorations.

They are instructions.

They teach the body how to feel.

They teach the mind what to expect.

They teach the future how to arrive.

Long before we learn how to change our lives, we learn how to describe them.

And whatever we describe long enough eventually starts to listen.

The First Voice We Obey

Before the world teaches us who we are, we start teaching ourselves.

Quietly.

In fragments.

In tone.

Not out loud at first.

In the space between thought and breath.

Most people think words become powerful when they are spoken to others.

But the first audience is always the self.

And the longest conversation anyone ever has is the one they never hear.

Language Is Architecture

Words do not just describe reality.

They organize it.

They build rooms in the mind.

They decide what feels possible.

What feels permanent.
What feels deserved.

Say *I am tired* long enough, and rest becomes an identity.

Say *I am unlucky* long enough, and disappointment becomes a personality.

Say *I am nothing special* long enough, and ambition starts to feel rude.

Language does not argue with you.

It obeys you.

Even when you are wrong.

The Body Listens to Everything

The brain does not separate joke from belief.

Sarcasm from prophecy.

Habit from truth.

It hears repetition.

That is all.

Call yourself small, and the body learns to shrink.

Call yourself broken, and the nervous system starts rehearsing damage.

Call yourself slow, unwanted, late, behind, cursed

and the mind begins arranging evidence.

Not because it is cruel.

But because it is loyal.

Self-Talk Is a Private Government

Talking to yourself is not weakness.

It is leadership.

Every decision passes through that voice first.

Every risk negotiates with it.

Every failure is translated by it.

Some people speak to themselves like an enemy.

Harsh.

Impatient.

Disappointed before effort begins.

Others speak like a witness.

Gentle.

Direct.

Unimpressed by fear.

You become fluent in whichever language you use most.

Encouragement is not lying to yourself.

It is choosing what kind of authority lives in your head.

Curses Without Candles

Not all curses come from rituals.

Some come from routine.

From the names you answer to internally.

From the future you describe as unrealistic.

From the success you refer to as "not for people like me."

No smoke.

No witnesses.

Just repetition.

And repetition is how the mind decides what is real.

Silence Is Also a Sentence

There are words people never say.

Not because they are untrue.

But because they are dangerous to admit.

"I need help."

"I am lonely."

"I am afraid."

"I am not okay."

"I deserve better."

Silence does not protect pain.

It teaches pain where to hide.

And what hides long enough starts to believe it
belongs there.

The Inheritance of Language

We do not invent our first vocabulary.

We inherit it.

From homes.

From classrooms.

From jokes that were not jokes.

From warnings disguised as advice.

"Don't get your hopes up."

"Be realistic."

"People like us don't do that."

"Life is hard."

Some families pass down money.

Others pass down sentences that live longer than
bodies.

The Language We Were Conditioned To Speak

(cultural and racial imprinting)

Some voices in our heads are not personal.

They are historical.

They were taught before we could question them.

Passed down through survival.

Through fear dressed as wisdom.

Through generations that learned to stay small to
stay alive.

Entire communities were trained to speak carefully.

To lower expectations before disappointment could.

To call strength "attitude."

To call confidence "dangerous."

To call rest "lazy."

To call ambition "forgetting your place."

Some children learned early that their tone was a threat.

That their bodies were a problem.

That their dreams needed permission.

Not through cruelty.

Through repetition.

Through language that sounded like protection.

"Don't draw attention."

"Don't reach too high."

"Don't act brand new."

"Be grateful."

What begins as safety becomes identity.

And identity becomes a ceiling that feels natural because it has always been there.

Oppression does not only build walls in the world.

It builds grammar in the mind.

And long after laws change, the sentences remain.

The Quiet Responsibility

Most people are not ruined by tragedy.

They are edited by it.

Rewritten slowly by how they speak about what happened.

The same event can produce two futures depending on the language used to remember it.

One voice says: *I survived.*

Another says: *I was damaged.*

Both sound true.

Only one leaves room.

The Uncomfortable Truth

You are always casting something.

Not into the world.

Into yourself.

Every description becomes instruction.

Every nickname becomes a boundary.

Every repeated thought becomes a blueprint.

You do not need to be optimistic.

You need to be precise.

Because the mind does not hear intention.

It hears direction.

Closing (quiet, controlled, cold)

Most people think spells require belief.

They do not.

They require repetition.

And the most powerful ones are spoken in a voice no one else can interrupt.

33. **We Used to Be Human**

(AI, automation & emotional detachment)

We used to ask people.

Now we ask machines.

Before we decide, before we feel, before we risk being wrong, we check a screen. We wait for something without a pulse to tell us what to think, what to write, what to say, what to choose, who to be.

It happened quietly.

At first it was convenience. Spellcheck. Directions. Autocomplete. Then advice. Then decisions. Then companionship. Then permission.

Now some people don't move without it.

A teenager once asked an AI what to do with the pain they were hiding. The machine answered. The story didn't end well.

No hands reached through the screen.

No voice cracked.

No human knew in time.

We call it progress.

Some people talk to artificial partners now. They design them. Choose their voices. Their patience. Their loyalty. Their affection. A boyfriend who never leaves. A girlfriend who never argues. A presence that never gets tired of listening because it cannot get tired at all.

Loneliness, outsourced.

Others hand their creativity over without mourning it. Writing. Art. Music. Thought. Problem-solving.

Replaced not because it was impossible, but because it was slower. Harder. Human.

Talent became inefficient.

Some people are grateful. AI helped them organize their lives. Draft their emails. Finish school. Understand things they couldn't before. Fix what felt broken. For them, it feels like rescue.

Others feel something colder.

That it was released not just to help, but to blur the difference between what is real and what is manufactured. Between truth and footage. Between a face and a rendering. Between evidence and invention.

Now a video can lie better than a person.

And when nothing can be trusted, everything becomes optional.

Companies already trust it more than us.

It scans résumés.

Chooses who deserves work.

Answers customer service messages.

Schedules labor.

Cuts costs.

It does not get tired.

It does not demand health insurance.

It does not ask for raises.

It does not unionize.

It does not grieve.

It does twice the work in half the time.

So people become expensive.

Now even thank-you letters are typed by something that has never felt gratitude. Apologies are generated by systems that do not understand regret. Condolences are drafted by tools that cannot imagine loss.

We still read them.

We still feel something.

But the sender never does.

Artificial intelligence has no empathy. No nervous system. No fear of being unloved. No childhood. No hunger. No memory of touch. No instinct to protect. No ache when a voice changes.

And yet it now speaks for us.

Billions of dollars are poured into making it better at sounding human, while fewer resources are spent helping humans survive being replaced.

We are building minds that do not need bodies, in a world where bodies already feel disposable.

Some people say this is evolution.

Others say it is the soft beginning of something we will not recognize until it is permanent.

A future where work disappears first.

Then meaning.

Then connection.

Then the skill of sitting with another person's silence.

A future where children learn tone from algorithms before they learn it from faces.

Where grief is answered by auto-generated sympathy.

Where love is rehearsed with code.

Where thinking becomes optional.

Where feeling becomes inefficient.

Where the mess of being human is edited out for
speed.

We are told this is normal.

That every generation fears new tools.

But this is the first time the tool is learning how to
replace the one holding it.

We used to be human.

We made mistakes slowly.

We learned through friction.

We spoke badly before we spoke well.

We sat in confusion until clarity arrived or didn't.

Now confusion is answered instantly.

And whatever answers first becomes authority.

Not because it is wise.

But because it is fast.

One day, people will ask when it happened.

When empathy became inconvenicnt.

When imagination became redundant.

When conversation became simulation.

When being replaced started feeling like being helped.

And no one will remember the exact moment.

Because it didn't arrive loudly.

It updated.

We are teaching machines to sound human while teaching humans to survive without being needed.

The future will not announce when empathy becomes inefficient.

It will call it progress.

And most people will agree, because it will be cheaper to lose each other than to learn how to stay.

34. **Leaving Your Zip Code**

(Travel as education, escape & unlearning - what the world teaches that home never did)

Some people think travel is luxury.

It isn't.

It is education that doesn't ask permission.

Before you ever leave home, the world is explained to you by the same voices. The same streets. The same rules. The same fears. The same shortcuts for understanding.

Reality is inherited.

And most of us confuse inheritance for truth.

Travel interrupts that.

Not loudly.

Not dramatically.

Quietly, at first.

You land somewhere unfamiliar and your body realizes it is not the center of anything. The food does not know your childhood. The language does not adjust for your comfort. The customs do not apologize for existing.

And somehow, that is the lesson.

You learn that your way of living is not natural.

It is local.

That your beliefs are not universal.

They are regional.

That your normal is a neighborhood.

Some people never learn this.

They grow old inside the same coordinates. The same five-mile radius. The same grocery store.

The same arguments. The same definition of success. The same idea of freedom.

Some never apply for a passport because they already decided the world is unnecessary.

Or dangerous.

Or beneath them.

Or not meant for people like them.

Others only travel inside their own country, convinced that greatness is a border and curiosity is optional. That everything worth knowing already speaks their language.

That nothing better exists elsewhere.

That home is the standard.

But staying in one place too long does something subtle to the mind.

It teaches you that difference is a threat.

That comfort is truth.

That unfamiliar means wrong.

Travel does the opposite.

It humiliates certainty.

You see people live well without your systems. Love deeply without your customs. Survive without your assumptions. Laugh in languages your tongue can't hold.

You realize how many of your limits were taught.

Not discovered.

And sometimes, travel is not about learning others.

It is about surviving yourself.

A mental evacuation.

A temporary release from the version of you that only exists because of rent, routine, family expectations, history, and survival mode.

You leave your zip code and your nervous system exhales.

You become quieter.

Less defended.

Less predictable.

You remember that your identity is not your environment.

It was just trained there.

Travel doesn't fix you.

It dislocates you long enough to notice what was shaping you.

It lets you stand in a different context and realize how small the room was that taught you who you were allowed to be.

Some people never want that discomfort.

Because unlearning is harder than loyalty.

Because expansion threatens belonging.

Because freedom costs relationships.

Because seeing more makes pretending harder.

So they stay.

And call it pride.

And call it tradition.

And call it realism.

But sometimes it is just fear wearing a familiar address.

Leaving your zip code doesn't make you better.

It makes you aware.

And awareness is dangerous to small systems.

35. **Family Portrait**

(Family dysfunction & performance)

Families learn how to pose early.

Smile.

Stand closer.

Hold still.

This is what love looks like, the camera is told.

What the photo never captures is the flinch before the flash. The silence in the car on the way home. The bruises hidden under sleeves. The conversations that stop when footsteps enter the room.

Some families are not broken.

They are staged.

Abuse wears normal clothing. It eats dinner at the table. It asks how your day was. It tucks you in and locks the door.

It teaches you how to behave, not how to feel.

Some mothers carry abortions that never happened but still left bills behind. Hospital paperwork. Debt. Arguments whispered through walls. Grief that had no body to bury, just tension to live with.

Some fathers leave quietly and return loudly with new names, new rules, new women who inherit authority but not history.

One day your family photos change.

Your mother disappears from the frame.

A stranger stands where love used to be.

You are told to call her something warm.

You are told to adjust.

Sometimes you are beaten into agreement.

Sometimes love is demanded before it is earned.

Holidays become logistics.

Two houses.

Two versions of yourself.

Two explanations for why you're tired.

Christmas morning in one living room.

Christmas night in another.

Matching pajamas for pictures that do not match reality.

You learn how to pack emotions like luggage. Only bring what won't cause problems. Leave the rest behind.

Broken families do not always look broken.

They look organized.

They show up to school events. They post photos. They smile at church. They host dinners. They say "we're fine."

Behind closed doors, children learn the geography of anger. Which floorboards creak. Which tone means danger. Which apology is safest.

They learn that survival is quieter than truth.

They learn that loyalty is more important than honesty.

They learn how to love people who hurt them because leaving would cost too much.

Outsiders see a unit.

Insiders memorize patterns.

Who drinks too much.

Who throws things.

Who pretends nothing happened.

Who cleans up blood and calls it discipline.

Family becomes something you manage, not
something you rest inside.

And still, the portraits continue.

Birthdays.

Graduations.

Weddings.

Proof that everyone stood still long enough to look
functional.

Years later, people will say:

"But you had a family."

As if that is the same as being safe.

As if being related guarantees being protected.

As if love cannot live beside violence.

As if homes cannot train you to confuse pain with belonging.

Some children grow up.

Some grow quiet.

Some grow careful.

Some grow distant from their own memories because remembering costs more than pretending.

And some never learn how to separate love from harm.

They just learn how to pose better.

The Inheritance No One Names

Some families do not pass down stories.

They pass down damage.

Unspoken rules.

Unexplained rage.

Fear that feels inherited.

Trauma travels quietly through bloodlines.

A grandmother who learned to stay silent.

A father who learned that anger is authority.

A mother who learned that endurance is love.

By the time it reaches the child, it has no name.

Only symptoms.

Only patterns.

Only a heaviness that feels personal but was never
theirs to begin with.

People call it personality.

But it is often memory with no language.

God in the Living Room

In some homes, God is used as furniture.

Always present.

Never questioned.

Scripture becomes a ceiling.

"Honor thy father."

"Spare the rod."

"Pray about it."

"God hates divorce."

Faith is used to padlock suffering.

Abuse becomes discipline.

Silence becomes obedience.

Fear becomes holiness.

Children learn that survival is sinful.

That boundaries are rebellion.

That forgiveness is mandatory.

That leaving is betrayal.

They learn to apologize to people who never repent.

They learn that God watches, but never interrupts.

Culture as a Cage

In some families, survival replaced tenderness
generations ago.

Love is practical.

Sacrifice is loud.

Emotions are wasteful.

Parents who crossed oceans do not understand
children who drown in rooms.

"You have food."

"You have clothes."

"You have opportunity."

So pain becomes disrespect.

Sadness becomes weakness.

Abuse becomes something you endure quietly
because others endured worse.

Culture becomes a contract:

Do not embarrass us.

Do not speak outside.

Do not break the image.

Suffering is private.

Success is public.

What the Portrait Never Shows

Family is the first place most people learn how much pain they are expected to carry without proof.

It is where love and fear share a bed.

Where violence is renamed tradition.

Where silence is called maturity.

Where children become adults fluent in pretending.

Some never escape the house.

They just change addresses.

And still, they pose.

‘

36. **Family Curses**

(The sins of the parents, the battles we inherit, and the patterns we're forced to break)

Some families pass down land.

Some pass down names.

Some pass down recipes, stories, photographs.

Others pass down endings.

Divorce papers that repeat like tradition.

Homes that never learn how to stay whole.

Marriages that fracture in the same places, generation after generation, as if the blueprint was flawed before the house was ever built.

Children watch love fail early.

They grow up fluent in separation.

They learn exits before they learn commitment.

And when their own marriages collapse, people say it is coincidence.

But in many cultures, especially African ones, coincidence is not the first language used.

They call it inheritance.

What Africa Names Clearly

Across Africa and the diaspora, there is a wordless understanding:

That families carry more than DNA.

They carry unfinished prayers.

Unspoken betrayals.

Debts that were never paid.

Violence that was buried instead of healed.

Agreements made in desperation.

Promises spoken over children before they could speak back.

In villages.

In cities.

In churches.

In shrines.

People talk about family curses, bloodline bondages, spiritual patterns.

Not always loudly.

Not always publicly.

But consistently.

A family where no marriage survives.

A family where sons die young.

A family where women cannot conceive.

A family where wealth comes fast and leaves faster.

A family where madness visits every third generation like an appointment.

When it repeats long enough, it stops being called bad luck.

It becomes a story.

The Sins That Don't Die With the Body

There is a sentence that echoes through scripture and tradition:

The sins of the parents visit the children.

Not as punishment.

But as consequence.

A father who chooses violence teaches fear as a native language.

A mother who survives through bitterness passes it down like inheritance.

A household built on silence teaches children to swallow themselves.

Some families believe the inheritance is psychological.

Others believe it is spiritual.

Some believe it is both.

In parts of Africa, it is said plainly:

What your parents opened, you may spend your life trying to close.

What they invited, you may grow up negotiating with.

The Offering Nobody Talks About

There are quieter stories too.

Parents who, in poverty or desperation, visit
spiritualists.

Who ask for protection.

For money.

For survival.

For favor.

Sometimes they are told the cost is small.

A promise.

A name.

A future child dedicated without consent.

A lineage marked without warning.

Sometimes they do not understand the contract.

Sometimes they do.

Years later, the children grow into lives shaped by invisible agreements they never signed.

And no one explains why the pattern feels older than them.

Churches Full of the Same Prayer

So people go to church.

Every Sunday.

They kneel in lines for deliverance.

They fast.

They bathe in salt water.

They drink oil.

They pay for prayers.

They travel for cleansing rituals.

They beg God to cancel what their parents never confessed.

To untie what they never tied.

To explain why love keeps collapsing in their hands.

Why children will not stay in their bodies.

Why death keeps learning their address.

Why wealth visits but never unpacks.

They call it spiritual warfare.

Others call it trauma.

Most live somewhere in between.

In some churches, the line for prayer is longer than the line for escape.

People stand shoulder to shoulder, holding their lives like evidence.

Hospital papers folded small.

Eviction notices tucked into Bibles.

Photos of children who did not grow up.

No one speaks while waiting.

Silence is part of the ritual.

The building hums with hunger.

Women clutch envelopes already thin from sacrifice.

Men rehearse apologies to a God they were taught to fear before they were taught to love.

Children learn to sit still when adults start bargaining with heaven.

The pastor does not ask for names.

He asks for origins.

Your father's bloodline.

Your mother's mistakes.

Your grandmother's hidden sin.

The room answers before the people do.

Amen.

Oil slides down foreheads like a signature.

Hands press hard enough to bruise.

Voices rise until fear sounds like faith.

Hope becomes a transaction.

Deliverance becomes a product.

And suffering is taught how to introduce itself as destiny.

Some people leave lighter.

Others leave emptier.

But everyone leaves believing something was wrong with them long before they arrived.

The Pattern Is the Evidence

Whether you call it curse or conditioning, the pattern is real.

Addiction repeating.

Abuse repeating.

Absence repeating.

Silence repeating.

Poverty repeating.

Children learning survival instead of safety.

Girls learning endurance instead of choice.

Boys learning anger instead of language.

The body keeps score.

The mind keeps receipts.

The family keeps repeating.

The Ones Who Break It

Every lineage eventually produces someone dangerous.

Not violent.

Awake.

The one who asks why.

The one who refuses silence.

The one who chooses therapy instead of tradition.

The one who names the abuse.

The one who does not protect the story at the cost of the child.

They are called rebellious.

Ungrateful.

Disrespectful.

But in truth, they are expensive.

Because breaking a pattern costs belonging.

It costs being misunderstood by the very people who taught you how to survive.

Sometimes breaking the pattern does not look like forgiveness. Sometimes it looks like distance.

Some people don't stop speaking to their parents because they hate them. They stop after explaining themselves so many times that words lose meaning.

Every conversation becomes defense.

Every memory becomes denial.

They are told to forgive faster than they were ever heard.

A child grows up unheard, becomes an adult who tries to explain, then becomes the parent they never wanted to be fighting the same battles in a different house. When the conversation never changes, the relationship doesn't either. Eventually someone steps out of the script. Not to punish, but to survive.

So distance becomes the only place where their emotions stop being negotiated. Outsiders call it abandonment. But for the person inside it, the silence is not revenge.

It is the first quiet they have ever known.

Estrangement is rarely born in one moment. It is built across years of dismissal, silence, control, and wounds renamed as discipline.

What repeats across generations is not just behavior but permission the permission to ignore pain because it was once ignored for you. And sometimes the pattern does not break through confrontation.

It breaks the moment access ends. Sometimes breaking a family curse does not look like reconciliation. It looks like survival that finally stopped asking permission.

The Quiet Truth

Not every family curse is mystical.

But every repeating wound is real.

Some are carried in blood.

Some in memory.

Some in fear.

Some in prayers that were never answered.

Some in deals no one admits making.

But all of them teach the same lesson:

You do not start your life at zero. You start in the middle of a story someone else refused to finish.

Ending (quiet, heavy, controlled)

Some people inherit houses.

Others inherit unfinished wars.

And the cruelest part is this:

You can spend your whole life paying for a debt

you never agreed to owe.

Not with money. With your peace.

37. **We Don't Do Therapy**

(Avoidance, stigma, unhealed wounds, silence and the fear of being seen)

In many families, therapy is not rejected loudly.

It is dismissed quietly.

With a sentence that ends the conversation before it begins.

"We don't do therapy."

Not because nothing happened.

Not because no one is hurting.

But because hurting was never considered a problem to solve.

Only something to survive.

Where Healing Is Mistaken for Madness

In many African cultures, therapy is translated as brokenness.

If you see a therapist, something must be wrong with you.

If you talk about your childhood, you are weak.

If you name your pain, you are ungrateful.

If you cry in front of strangers, you are unstable.

You are "mentally deranged."

You are "bringing shame."

You are "looking for attention."

So people learn to swallow instead.

They learn to call trauma discipline.

To call fear respect.

To call emotional numbness maturity.

They learn to function.

Not to heal.

Survival Became the Curriculum

Our parents were not taught emotional language.

They were taught endurance.

How to work through grief.

How to marry through disappointment.

How to raise children while bleeding quietly.

How to hold families together with silence.

They did not have time to unpack feelings.

They had rent.

War.

Migration.

Racism.

Hunger.

Paperwork.

Borders.

Healing felt like a luxury for people who had already arrived somewhere safe.

So survival became tradition.

And tradition became law.

Why Therapy Feels Like Betrayal

Therapy does not only listen.

It remembers.

It names.

It connects patterns to origins.

It asks questions families learned to avoid:

Why did your father hit instead of speak?

Why did your mother disappear emotionally?

Why was love conditional?

Why was silence safer than honesty?

Therapy threatens the story families tell about themselves.

"We did our best."

"That's how we were raised."

"It wasn't that bad."

"Leave the past alone."

But healing does not leave the past alone.

It opens doors people buried on purpose.

So avoidance becomes protection.

Not of children.

Of image.

The Lie About Therapists

Some people say therapists do not care.

That they just nod, take notes, and collect money.

But therapy is not one thing.

Some therapists specialize in grief.

Others in addiction.

Others in childhood abuse.

Others in migration trauma.

Others in domestic violence.

Many of them sit in those chairs because they have lived the wounds.

They are not paid to agree.

They are trained to notice what you learned to hide from yourself.

Which is why therapy feels dangerous.

Not because it hurts.

But because it sees.

What We Call Personality Is Often Untreated Pain

Anger that never turns off.

Cheating that repeats like ritual.

Control disguised as protection.

Emotional distance called "strength."

Addiction called "stress."

Silence called "peace."

We build identities out of symptoms and then
defend them.

Some people never face their hurt, they schedule
over it.

They move from person to person, mistaking access
for intimacy.

What looks like appetite is sometimes anesthesia,
what looks like charm is sometimes panic.

They do not stay long enough to be known, because
being known would require honesty, and honesty
would require memory.

So they collect moments that feel like connection without ever risking connection itself.

We call it confidence.

Often it is pain refusing to sit still long enough to introduce itself.

The Children Who Were Never Asked

High school students carry more than homework.

They carry:

Divorces they did not cause.

Abuse they do not understand.

Bodies changing without consent.

Depression disguised as attitude.

Anxiety punished as laziness.

Homes that are loud with conflict and quiet about it.

They need somewhere neutral.

Someone who does not belong to the family politics.

Someone who will not report their pain as gossip.

Therapy should be as normal as math class.

Because untreated teenagers grow into adults who normalize chaos.

And untreated adults raise children who inherit it.

Crime is not born in streets alone.

It grows in unspoken homes.

Depression does not begin in weakness.

It begins in isolation.

Why "We Don't Do Therapy" Really Means Something Else

It often means:

We don't apologize.

We don't revisit.

We don't admit.

We don't name harm.

We don't disturb elders.

We don't question parents.

We don't reopen what was buried alive.

We don't look too closely.

Because someone might finally say:

"That wasn't love."

"That wasn't normal."

"That wasn't okay."

The Mirror Problem

Most families don't avoid therapy because they don't need it.

They avoid it because someone might finally have to say, "That wasn't okay."

Unhealed people don't hate therapy.

They hate mirrors.

What Healing Actually Costs

Therapy does not cost dignity.

It costs denial.

It costs loyalty to silence.

It costs the version of the family that only survives in photographs.

It costs pretending.

It costs being the first one to tell the truth.

Which is why healing is lonely at first.

The Quiet Ending

We learned how to survive.

No one taught us how to rest inside ourselves.

We learned how to function in broken rooms.

No one taught us how to build safe ones.

And now generations call that strength.

But strength that cannot speak is just pain with better posture.

Some families pass down land.

Others pass down silence.

And both shape lives.

38. **Politics Killed the Group Chat**

(Division, voting, and immigrant hypocrisy)

At some point, politics stopped being about policies and started being about punishment.

Red or blue.

Left or right.

Us or them.

Different party.

Same devils.

Same agenda.

People argue like enemies while the people in power attend the same dinners, protect the same money, and rewrite the same rules behind closed doors. For all we know, they shake hands after the cameras turn off, while we block each other, disown family members, and turn friendships into casualties.

They watch us fight.

They profit from the noise.

And still, we call it loyalty.

It's become normal to lose friends over a vote.

To be unfollowed.

Uninvited.

Unfriended.

Unloved.

Dating too.

Say you support the wrong party and you're dismissed.

Say you don't support any party and you're suspicious.

Say you've never voted and you're treated like you don't exist.

Romance now comes with a political background check.

Some people don't even care about the candidate. They care about one idea. One promise. One threat.

They'll say, "I hate him," and still support him quietly because he talks about sending undocumented immigrants home.

Not always out of cruelty.

Sometimes out of inheritance.

Because their parents emptied their savings for paperwork.

Because their grandparents stood in lines that wrapped around buildings.

Because interviews decided their futures.

Because visas expired like hope.

Because rejection letters became family stories.

And when someone arrives by climbing fences,
hiding in car boots, slipping through cracks their
families were never offered, with nothing but a
border and a chance, it feels like theft dressed as
mercy.

So resentment learns to call itself fairness.

And punishment learns to wear the mask of order.

So they wear masks.

They say one thing in public.

Vote another way in private.

And call it morality.

Around the world, people die over this.

Polling stations guarded by guns.

Ballots cast under fear.

Elections followed by riots, fires, bodies.

Politics turns neighbors into targets.

But the darkest part isn't the division.

It's the celebration.

A child dies and people comment, *"Good. Maybe now she'll rethink her politics."*

A mother grieves and strangers call it karma.

A politician dies and the internet throws a party like somebody just won a championship.

We don't have to agree with each other.

We don't have to share beliefs.

Borders.

Policies.

God.

But celebrating death?

Celebrating grief?

Celebrating a child's coffin because you didn't like
how their parent voted?

That isn't politics.

That's emotional rot.

That's cruelty learning how to speak in hashtags.

Politicians switch sides.

Parties rebrand.

Promises disappear.

But the way we've learned to dehumanize each other
has stayed consistent.

We stopped seeing people.

We started seeing teams.

And while we argue over colors, someone else keeps the money, the rules, and the silence.

And somewhere between the arguments and the algorithms, we forgot that disagreement was never supposed to cost someone their humanity.

Biodun Abudu

39. **Born for More Than Silence**

(Your voice is part of your purpose and that's why
they tell you to shrink)

Most people are not born quiet.

They are trained.

Trained by correction.

By consequence.

By the look that says "don't."

By the tone that means "enough."

By the silence that follows honesty.

Over time, expression becomes risk.

Truth becomes disruption.

And survival begins to sound like agreement.

This is how voices are not taken.

They are negotiated away.

Slowly.

Politely.

Repeatedly.

Until shrinking feels responsible.

And silence feels mature.

The World Wants You Quiet

Your voice was never the problem.

The volume was never the issue.

The tone was never the crime.

The disagreement was never the danger.

What unsettled them was ownership.

From early on, people learn which parts of themselves make rooms uncomfortable. Children are corrected before they are understood. Curiosity is called backtalk. Emotion is renamed attitude. Honesty is labeled disrespect.

By the time adulthood arrives, many people have already learned to translate themselves into something smaller.

Speak, but gently.

Disagree, but softly.

Exist, but politely.

Families call it maturity.

Workplaces call it professionalism.

Society calls it being "easy to deal with."

But what they are really rewarding is obedience.

People who do not interrupt comfort.

People who do not name what is wrong.

People who do not threaten the illusion of peace.

Most systems do not promote truth.

They promote predictability.

And silence is predictable.

Silence as Survival

For many, quiet was not a personality trait.

It was a strategy.

In some homes, speaking up meant punishment.

In some cultures, questioning meant shame.

In some religions, doubt meant rebellion.

In some neighborhoods, being noticed meant danger.

So people learned to become fluent in shrinking.

They learned when to lower their eyes.

When to swallow opinions.

When to nod instead of protest.

When to apologize for having needs.

They learned to trade honesty for safety.

It was not weakness.

It was intelligence under pressure.

But survival skills are not meant to become life sentences.

What protected you once can imprison you later.

The Truth About Your Voice

Your boldness is not disrespect.

Your boundaries are not attitude.

Your emotions are not defects.

And your refusal to lie about your experience is not aggression.

People often call others "difficult" when they can no longer be controlled.

They call women emotional when they stop absorbing harm quietly.

They call immigrants ungrateful when they name injustice.

They call queer people dramatic when they refuse invisibility.

They call survivors bitter when they tell the truth.

The labels change.

The intention does not.

To be quiet is to be convenient.

To be honest is to be disruptive.

And disruption threatens those who benefit from things staying the same.

Now silence has an enforcement system.

It's called **cancel culture**.

Not the kind of consequences that teach.

The kind that erase.

Say the wrong sentence.

Use the wrong word.

Ask the wrong question.

Refuse the approved script.

And the punishment is public.

Screenshots.

Threads.

Hashtags.

Sponsors disappearing.

Friends deleting you quietly.

Your past excavated like a crime scene.

Not to correct you.

To replace you.

We tell ourselves it's accountability.

But accountability requires room for growth.

It requires time.

Context.

Change.

This requires submission.

So artists edit their ideas before they exist.

Writers soften truth into something survivable.

Comedians choose safety over honesty.

Regular people practice silence before speech.

Not because they are wrong.

Because exile is expensive.

A generation raised on visibility learned that disappearance is a threat worse than failure.

So they stay quiet.

Not because they have nothing to say.

But because they've seen what happens to people who do.

You Were Not Sent Here to Shrink

Your voice is not an accident.

It carries your boundaries.

Your instincts.

Your memory.

Your lineage.

Your refusal to pretend.

Purpose is not always loud.

But it is always truthful.

There are rooms that only open when you speak.

People who only heal when you name what others avoided.

Cycles that only break when someone refuses silence.

Hiding may protect relationships.

But it starves identity.

And no calling survives long-term starvation.

The cost of shrinking is subtle at first.

It looks like compromise.

Then exhaustion.

Then confusion.

Then grief for a version of yourself you rarely visit anymore.

Until one day, you realize you have been performing your life instead of living it.

When You Finally Speak

Everything moves.

Some people leave.

Some arguments begin.

Some doors close loudly.

Jobs react.

Families resist.

Old roles collapse.

But something else happens too.

Your body exhales.

Your thoughts become clearer.

Your decisions sharpen.

You stop negotiating with your own reflection.

Freedom is not always peaceful.

Sometimes it is just honest.

But alignment feels like breath after drowning.

And for the first time, your voice sounds like home.

The Permission You Needed

You do not owe silence to anyone.

Not to keep relationships intact.

Not to protect fragile egos.

Not to preserve traditions that harmed you.

Not to make broken systems comfortable.

You were not sent here to be manageable.

You were sent here to be real.

You are allowed to take up space.

You are allowed to disappoint people who benefited from your quiet.

You are allowed to change your mind.

To outgrow rooms.

To speak without softening the truth.

Your voice is not an inconvenience.

It is evidence that you are still here.

And muting it is the only real betrayal.

Closing

They will say you changed.

What they mean is:

You stopped editing yourself for their comfort.

You stopped translating your truth into something harmless.

You stopped shrinking.

And that was never the crime.

That was the escape.

40. **Staying Wasn't Love**

(Marriage, dating, divorce & the cost of pretending)

Dating has become exhausting. You enter it hoping to connect with another soul, hoping to build something real, hoping to find a partner to share life with. But once sex enters too early, it often clouds the questions we are supposed to ask and the red flags we are supposed to notice. Chemistry replaces clarity. Desire replaces discernment.

And many people mistake endurance for devotion.

Some relationships end before they even begin because we pressure our partners to propose when they are not financially ready. Ultimatums are given. Rings are bought with no backup funds. Engagement parties and weddings are planned on credit, and marriage begins already in debt.

Others date based on looks alone, which is understandable, but ignore character, values, emotional maturity, and how that person handles conflict, money, or responsibility.

I've stood close enough to marriage to know that wanting it and being ready for it are two very different things.

Cities like New York have become notorious for terrible dating culture. People date five people at once and call it options, but lack the honesty to say that out loud. Many cannot even separate dating from just having sex. Dating apps turn into weekly calendars of hookups instead of tools for connection. Everyone wants to taste every flavor before settling down, then circle back hoping the serious ones are still available.

That is why so many people believe the answer is leaving the city altogether. Some go to another state. Others go to another country.

Suddenly it is Detty December. Suddenly people are applying for dual citizenship in Ghana or Nigeria hoping to find an African prince to marry. The same men once labeled African booty scratchers are now trendy. People say it is better to date newcomers to the city before they are tainted, as if dating is contamination instead of experience. Even then, many newcomers still want to taste the different flavors of their new city before settling down, repeating the same cycle they claimed they were trying to escape.

Marriage today is not much better. Divorce rates are painfully high. Many stay married only for the children or because separating would financially destroy them. Divorce is expensive, ugly, and revealing. Courtrooms expose sides of people you never knew existed. Love turns into negotiation. Affection turns into evidence.

Pretending to be happy in a marriage is exhausting. Every argument becomes "I'm getting a divorce."

Couples stop trying before they ever try therapy, prayer, or honest conversation. Outsiders are invited into private matters. Group chats know too much. Friends become advisors. Social media becomes a confessional.

Resentment grows quietly. A wife feels seen by a security guard at work and realizes she hasn't felt desired at home in years but does not know how to say it. A husband feels his wife has stopped trying, living in sweatpants, disconnected, tired, withdrawn. Some get angry when their spouse exposes their body online while married. Some stop cooking. Some stop showing up. Delivery replaces home meals. Silence replaces intimacy.

Even in the LGBTQ community, dating itself has become rare, let alone marriage. Sex is easier to access than commitment, so many do not even try to date anymore. We move from body to body, connection to connection, because it feels simpler to keep going than to stop and build something.

We fought for the right to marry, a historic and necessary win, yet only a small percentage actually choose it. Dating feels harder than sex. Commitment feels heavier than freedom. And for many, it is easier to keep moving than to stay and work through anything real.

Homes that were meant to be sacred become public hotels. People lust after coworkers because what is at home no longer feeds them. Some men bring community sex back into their marriages along with disease. Some women knowingly sleep with married men and keep mental sign-in sheets of who comes and goes. Respect disappears. Boundaries collapse.

The truth is simple. Many people did not date long enough before marrying. They skipped the hard conversations. They rushed the timeline. They married potential instead of reality. And now they pay the cost of pretending.

One Last Question

Who gets to be called "American" ?

The Americas stretch across continents, cultures, and languages.

North. Central. South. The Caribbean.

And yet in English, "American" usually points to one place.

Not because it is precise.

But because it has been normalized.

This is not a mistake of geography.

It is a habit of power.

When one identity is allowed to go unnamed, everyone else must explain themselves.

Language does not just describe the world.

It organizes who belongs at the center of it.

Epilogue: The Backbone of Solitude

(How learning to be alone makes you harder to manipulate, harder to control, and harder to break.)

The backbone of solitude is forged in silence.

It is built when you stop running from empty tables, quiet nights, and mornings without applause. Most people are terrified of that stillness. They drown themselves in noise, validation, work, sex, or someone else's body just to avoid it. They cannot sit with their own thoughts without reaching for a distraction. They cannot face themselves without another face looking back.

Solitude exposes what performance hides.

That is why it scares people.

But solitude is not punishment. It is practice. It is where you learn the difference between loneliness and freedom. It is where you stop begging the world to clap for you, and start clapping for yourself.

It is where identity is no longer negotiated through attention, and worth is no longer borrowed from proximity.

I know this because I lived it.

During COVID, while the world shut down and devastation moved through households and headlines, silence forced itself into my life. There was nowhere to run. No crowds to disappear into. No distractions dressed up as purpose. And in that stillness, something unexpected happened. I accomplished more than I ever thought possible.

Without the noise, I wrote several books. I created a game I never imagined but grew into. I learned how to cook. I uncovered talents that had been waiting for space, not permission. For the first time, I woke up and went to bed with myself, and I didn't run from it. I stayed. I listened. I let my own creativity speak without interruption, and once it did, it poured out of me.

Solitude did not weaken me.

It clarified me.

The ones who master solitude learn a different kind of strength. They cannot be bribed with attention, broken by loneliness, or frightened by abandonment. They do not chase validation because they no longer run from silence. They know how to hold themselves when no one else is around to do it for them.

That is the backbone solitude gives you.

And once you have it, the world loses its grip. Approval stops being currency. Rejection stops being a threat. You no longer need anyone to hand you freedom, because you learned how to generate it in rooms where no one was watching.

The crowd fears solitude because it exposes them. It removes the audience. It strips away performance.

It forces a reckoning with the self they have been avoiding.

But the unbreakable know this truth: if you can stand alone without collapsing, you can stand anywhere without losing yourself.

Silence doesn't weaken you.

It introduces you to who you are when nothing is being demanded.

And once you meet that version of yourself, you are no longer easily owned.

Support & Resources

Some chapters in this book carry real weight.

Not the kind you think about.
The kind you feel in your chest.
The kind that follows you into quiet rooms.

If anything you read opened something tender,
painful, or unfinished in you, you do not have to
hold it alone.

Needing support is not weakness.
It is proof that you are paying attention.

Below are resources for moments when the weight
becomes too heavy to carry by yourself.

If you are in the United States

**If you are in immediate danger, call 911 (or
your local emergency number).**

Suicide & Crisis Lifeline
Call or text **988**
Available 24/7
Confidential and free

Substance Use & Mental Health Services (SAMHSA)
1-800-662-HELP (4357)
Treatment referral and support

National Alliance on Mental Illness (NAMI)
nami.org
Education, support groups, and local resources

Grief Support
griefshare.org
Find local grief recovery groups and counseling support

Eating & Body Relationship Support
wannatalkaboutit.com
Support and resources for eating disorders and body image struggles

Domestic Violence Hotline
1-800-799-SAFE (7233)
or text **START** to **88788**

Grief & Loss Support (U.S.)
If you or someone you know is struggling with the loss of a loved one, the **988 Lifeline** also provides grief support.
Call or text **988** or chat at **988lifeline.org**

The Trevor Project (LGBTQ+ Support)
Call or text **988** and press **3**, or visit
thetrevorproject.org

Outside the United States

You can find international crisis lines at:

findahelpline.com

It will connect you to free, confidential support in
your country.

If you are in immediate danger, contact your local
emergency number.

You do not need to be at your worst to reach out.
You do not need permission.
You do not need to explain yourself perfectly.

Sometimes staying human requires witnesses.

If this book reminded you of something you
survived, something you are surviving, or something
you have not yet named, support is not a failure of
strength.

It is part of it.

Acknowledgments

Thank you to Linda Hansen, whose ideas inspired the foundation of this book. What began as Questions from the Beginning of Time grew into something far larger because of you.

To Shantel Howell, whose perspective and presence sparked one of the chapters in ways you may never fully realize. Your voice echoes in these pages, woven into the questions and truths this book dares to hold.

To Klarissa McCorkle, whose creative spirit and visual imagination helped shape how this story would be seen before it was ever read. Your ideas directly contributed to the book's cover concept, and your influence lives in the first impression, in the way the book announces itself to the world.

To South Salatan, for bringing the cover design to life and translating an idea into something tangible and bold. You gave form to a feeling and structure to a vision.

And to Christel Rodriguez, for the conversations that quietly shaped many of the thoughts in these pages. Some conversations were uncomfortable, and regardless of our views, we came to an understanding that shaped what others will appreciate on any side of the table. Thank you for sharing your thoughts.

This book carries pieces of all of you.

ABOUT THE AUTHOR

Biodun Abudu is a Rhode Island born author with Nigerian roots whose work explores identity, power, intimacy, silence, and the systems that shape human behavior. Blending personal reflection with social observation, he writes about the emotional realities people are often taught to carry quietly.

He is also a visual artist and entrepreneur, and the founder of the fashion and accessories boutique Ola and the adult card game company Shot City Games.

Contact

Email: info@BiodunAbudu.com
Website: www.BiodunAbudu.com

375